You Got This:
Healing Through Divorce

You Got This: Healing Through Divorce

Whitney Boole, M.A., LMFT

ISBN:
978-1-7338490-1-2 (e)
978-1-7338490-0-5 (sc)

First Edition: March 15, 2019

For Riley, Wesley and Wren for all that you teach me every day and for your patience with my imperfection. You keep me humble and make me want to be more. May you always know how loved you are by both of your parents.

CONTENTS

Introduction

Fear, exhaustion, sadness, anger, and even outright terror may pave the start of your divorce. It did mine. It makes so much sense and it may feel like the end of the world right now. I get it. I really do. That's why I am writing this.

Have a baby and the world embraces you, tells you what to expect. Get a divorce, best of luck. Most people will look at you with pity and say, "I'm so sorry" and then avoid you because the conversation is too uncomfortable, and they don't know what else to say.

I'm not sorry. Divorce is one of the hardest things I have ever been through, but nobody does it on a whim. When you get divorced, you get divorced because it was absolutely necessary.

Divorce is not the end of the world. Depending on what you have been through, it can be the start of a much better one. I went through this journey myself, and having come through the other side, I believe this whole-heartedly for myself, for you, for anyone else going through it.

I'm a therapist who specializes in working with trauma. Divorce is absolutely traumatic — it upends everything, leaving you to question the very foundation of who you are and who you thought you would be.

My background as a therapist has fueled and informed this book, but the part of me writing this book is the part that's been in the trenches like you. I was bound and determined to come through this divorce with a life far better and happier than the one I left. I needed it — for me and for my kids. And I want to share that with you because I believe everybody going through a divorce should get a happily ever after. When you get married, people wish you all the best in your new life. Divorce should be the same because if anything, you need that sentiment now more than ever.

So, let me be the first to congratulate you on your divorce and wish you love, laughter, and happiness in your new life.

I didn't want to just survive my divorce. I wanted to thrive through it. It is possible. I know it is because I did it. I am doing it. And so can you.

There are exercises woven into the book to help you work through this journey. I recommend creating a file on your computer or handwriting in a journal to complete the exercises. Make sure that the journal or document is not accessible to anyone but you. Your children, if you have any, should never see any of this.

This is your private journey — it's just for you.

If you are not sure you want to get a divorce:

If you're on the fence about whether to get a divorce, *please don't read this*. The decision to end a marriage is not an easy one and this book will not help you make it. If you're not sure, go to therapy, do some soul-searching, and see if your marriage can be salvaged. A marriage that weathers the storm is a gift and totally irreplaceable. Don't underestimate the value. If it cannot be saved, pick up this book again when you've come to that conclusion.

A note to men and gay couples:

This is not a man-bashing book or a heteronormative book. I use pronouns based on my own gender and sexuality because it feels weird to write it otherwise. Besides, no matter how much empathy I have for men or LGBTQ individuals, I am not a man or LGBTQ and I have not walked this path in those shoes. However, the challenges of divorce do not discriminate based on gender or orientation and I welcome you, if you are a man or LGBTQ, to read this book and feel empowered as well. Don't be offended by the pronouns — I'm not attacking men or excluding LGBTQ individuals, although I do share how my experience with divorce has jaded my perceptions of men in ways that are unfair. You may feel the same way about women sometimes and I totally get that. If you're a man or identify as LGBTQ and you're reading this, welcome. Just flip the pronouns or adjust it as needed and try not to personalize the pronouns.

SECTION 1:

A NEW ONCE UPON A TIME

Moving on, letting go and saving your SELF

THIS IS THE DAY YOU MAKE YOURSELF A PRIORITY. RIGHT HERE, RIGHT NOW.

You don't have to agree with everything I write in this book. I take no offense if you read a chapter and decide it's not for you. But this chapter, this one, you really need to take in. It's important.

There's an embarrassing secret about my marriage that I don't share often and it's something I am not proud of — it's not about him, it's about me. At every revelation of betrayal and the pain my ex-husband inflicted on me during our marriage, I comforted <u>him</u>. I worried about <u>him</u>, I took care of <u>him</u>, I cared for <u>him</u>. And the truth is that I abandoned <u>me</u> in doing that. This was not because I was kind or selfless. It's because I was too scared to connect with what I was feeling and how I was hurting. It's because I didn't value my own pain as much as caring for the pain of others. It's because I couldn't tolerate making myself a priority — it felt selfish.

When life was at its most painful during my marriage, I comforted him and ignored myself. And here's the kicker, I cannot blame him for that.

Neglecting myself was all my doing. He didn't make me do that, he didn't ask me to do that. It was me. I did that. Now, I get to do it differently. And I am. I don't take care of him, I don't think about him, I don't worry about him in any capacity except in terms of how it impacts our kids. I make myself a priority, treating myself as though I am worthy of that because I am. And so are you. We are worthy. And even in relationship, I am careful to make sure that I don't lose myself the way I did before.

If you're reading this book, it's time to make yourself a priority. It's time to take care of you and focus on what you need to heal. Your family, your friends, and anyone who loves you wants that for you. No, you're not selfish for taking care of you. You need to take care of you to show up for others.

It starts with you. Right here, right now.

YOU ARE NOT CRAZY. THIS IS HARD.

Going through a divorce is likely to trigger anxiety, depression, sadness, frustration, confusion and a swirl of conflicting and maddening emotions that can be absolutely overwhelming. Your reality has just taken a gut punch and you're having to reconsider everything. This divorce impacts your living situation, your relationships with your children, your relationships with your family (yours and his too), your relationships with friends, and even your relationship with yourself. It's a lot.

Additionally, your ex who was once your committed and trusted life partner may behave in ways that confound and alarm you. I remember early on feeling scared of my ex like perhaps he might hurt me when he had no history of violence or abuse and I had absolutely no rational reason to think he might hurt me. I felt like a paranoid lunatic, and yet my fear was genuine and real.

If you are feeling crazy, rest assured, you have every right and reason to feel this way.

And you are absolutely not alone. I felt intensely crazy at several points over the course of my divorce, and I have a Master's Degree in Clinical Psychology. I feel you. This is hard. The craziness will fade but it may take time and work to get there.

THIS IS WAR. TRAIN. GET STRONG.

My therapist told me early on that this was war. Naive me. I thought to myself, "No, it's not. We will be kind. We will not go to war." But I did not understand.

Retrieving yourself from a marriage in which you've become so entwined with another human being is a battle like nothing you've ever seen before. I am not talking about fights over finances or custody, although that stuff can be brutal too. I am talking about the fight to reclaim the pieces of you that you forgot existed or never even knew were there.

This fight is a fight to salvage yourself, your sense of calm, your dreams and hopes for the future, your routines and ways of living, your traditions for yourself and for your family. The money and custody, that's another story. You can't do any of that if you haven't fought for yourself first.

The day I ended my marriage, I felt gutted and raw. Who would I be? How would I move forward? What would my life look like? It broke me open, and while I knew it was exactly what I needed and there was no other way, it hurt with an intensity that frightened me. I didn't only feel emotionally raw — the pain was physical too. My whole body ached.

Everything you imagined the world would be has just been decimated. You have to reinvent all of it for yourself without the husband you chose in it. You're on your own. And depending on how long your marriage was, it may have been a long time since you've been this alone. I get how scary that is. I was married fifteen years and in that relationship for twenty. I wasn't single in my twenties at all and had only a few months left in my thirties.

Even in kindness, divorce is war. You are at war. When you are trying to make a marriage work, you take the armor down and try to connect. Going through a divorce, you put the armor up and keep yourself safe.

When I first realized my broken marriage could not be salvaged and that I could not stop my husband's lies and betrayals, I cried. I cried a lot. I didn't sleep much. I didn't want to eat. I didn't feel strong. But I wanted to be strong.

I needed to be strong.

The night I told him that he needed to get out, I cried until two a.m. and then woke up the next morning, tired and weak, and I ran.

I was not a runner. I did not run fast. I did not run well. I did not even love to run. But I loved to feel strong. The more I ran, the more mornings that I got up at the crack of dawn and carried myself out the door, the stronger I felt. I did yoga sometimes. Hot yoga, with half-naked smelly people in a room heated super-hot. And when I did it, I felt strong. I went to the batting cages and hit balls. It felt good to hit things. I went to kickboxing classes and punched heavy bags. The instructor asked me who I was so mad at. It felt good.

I was training for a fight that I didn't even understand. At the time, I couldn't wrap my head around any of it. All I could do is cultivate my strength.

If you are going through a divorce, you need your strength too. Even if your divorce is kinder than mine, you will need the fight to reclaim your sense of self.

To get through this, you need to be stronger than you've ever been before. Whether it's running or meditation or weights or yoga or swimming or dancing or whatever - go do it. Find all the strength you can even when you think there's none left. Connect to your body, your physical strength first. The rest will follow. It's tempting to curl up in bed and eat your way through this, but it will leave you feeling weak and sick.

Thrive. You never needed him to be the person you want to be. Fight and reclaim the pieces of you that were so wrapped up in your dreams for the future with him.

You can do this. I know that you can. And if you believe it, you will.

Eat well, exercise, sleep - these are the three things that you can do to train. As a therapist, I also know that these are the three things that help balance your brain chemistry and keep you feeling even. But don't do it to balance your brain chemistry. That is too reasonable for how you feel right now.

Do it because you want to come out of this stronger and fiercer than ever before. Do it because you need your fight and you are worth fighting for.

If it feels like there's a dark cloud hanging above you that you can't get out from under, fight like hell to get to the other side of it. If you can't, find a good therapist or someone to help drag you through. There is no weakness in getting help. I did. Get the help you need before you sink and then get up and train.

It will pay off, no matter how much it hurts. I know. I have been there.

Exercise: Find strength and create action.

What activities make you feel strong? What does strength look like and feel like to you? If this is challenging, think back to times in your life when you have felt strong — what were you doing then? Or maybe it's an activity you've never tried but looks like something strong people do — why not try it?

Next, create a concrete action plan. Commit to an activity that feels like strength and go do it. Make the plan concrete — when, where and how are you going to do it. Calendar it. Make it happen.

CREATE A SANCTUARY.

When my husband moved out, I made him take our old bed with him. It was not negotiable. I wanted everything cleared out of the bedroom we shared together.

My bedroom was not a calm place to sleep anymore. It was a reminder of the betrayals I had suffered, the pain I had endured. I hated everything about it - the pictures that hung on the walls like artifacts of my broken marriage, the bedding that smelled of the decayed life we had together, the bed that was ugly and heavy to me now, the mattress itself that swallowed me up and had a hole in the space beside me where a husband once was. They were all reminders of a former self and a former life that brought me no comfort at all. And I needed comfort, more than anything.

Everything had to go. As soon as possible.

As the day of his move approached, I enjoyed picking out a new bed and finding new bedding. Our king bed was too big for me. The simple white queen bed I found on sale was just the right size. I created a room that felt like a breath of fresh air. Honestly, it was simple and clean. I went Marie Kondo on it as I had in my marriage and got rid of everything that did not spark joy. (If you have not read Marie Kondo's *The Life Changing Magic of Tidying Up,* I highly recommend it). I threw out clothes that didn't feel right to me, belts that I hadn't worn in years, and shoes that looked like they belonged to former versions of myself that no longer existed. The artifacts on the wall looked at home in the trash bags I took to Goodwill.

I cleaned out my room until all that was left was my brand new clean white bed with my new beige and blue striped linen duvet, a nightstand for my books, and drawers with only the clothes that bring me joy. I wash my sheets with lavender dryer sheets so that my bed is always scented like a spa. The simplicity of it brings me comfort.

This space is sacred to me now. It is mine. Anything that does not spark joy, most notably my ex, will not come into this space. My bed is a magical fluffy cloud — it exists solely for me. My bedroom is the place I escape to at the end of the day. My retreat. My safe place. I needed that to get through this.

Creating a retreat is important, especially if you were traumatized by your marriage as I was in mine. Creating a retreat for myself is one of the best things I did for me. You don't have to spend a lot of money to create your sanctuary — a half hour on Pinterest will give you a flood of ideas on a budget if that's important. Pieces of nature or nostalgia can bring immense comfort. I have a jar of seashells my kids and I collected on vacation and a box of mementos from my childhood.

Consider your sanctuary an investment in you. Did you always wish he would light candles for you in your bedroom after a relaxing bubble bath? Guess what, you can make that happen. Your sanctuary is magical and the person who brings the magic to it is you.

I love my bedroom. I keep it clean and ordered and I look forward to the end of the day when I can rest there.

Your retreat may be your bedroom. It may be somewhere else. Bedrooms work well because it's the first thing we see at the start of the day and where we retreat when the day is done. Whatever it is for you, create a sanctuary, some place that leaves you feeling safe and calm. Take down any photographs of your ex-husband — they no longer belong in your safe haven. If you are not ready to toss them, put them in a box, label it, and put it away where you don't have to see it right now. Hang photos that bring you joy. You don't have to break the bank — a coat of fresh paint or a single picture that feels meaningful goes a long way.

Don't only take away the pieces of your life that you are letting go of — fill your space with the pieces of your life you want to embrace. Your sanctuary is not a hole that needs to be filled. You are enough here. You are safe here. You are loved here. To be honest, there's not all that much in my bedroom. I like it that way. There is plenty of space for me.

You will need your sanctuary to get through this. Take solace in it. Leave only what brings you joy there.

Exercise: Create your sanctuary — imagine it and build it.

Close your eyes and imagine a safe space in your home. What does it look like? How does it feel? What does it smell like? Notice what comes up for you and what you see in that space. Consider artifacts from childhood or nature as anchors. Notice what brings you joy and consider letting go of all that doesn't. What would that be like?

Next, make it happen. If money is tight, do it on a budget. Clear out everything that feels heavy or a reminder of the pain you've suffered and make space for the things that bring you joy.

Make your sanctuary a place of nurture and calm and comfort. Enjoy it. Retreat there when you need to.

BREATHE.

I give people lots of techniques to manage anxiety, stress, and grief. One simple technique stands above the rest and it's going to sound silly but believe me it's not:

Breathing.

Really, breathing is the most important thing you do every day — if you didn't, you would die. Nothing is more critical to your well-being. We take it for granted. But there is power in every breath you take, especially when you learn how to harness it. My clients are often surprised by how powerful the simple act of mindful deep belly breathing can be.

When you breathe, you oxygenate your blood. You take in life-sustaining oxygen and breathe out all that no longer serves you. I invite you to strengthen your relationship with your breath. If you let it, breathing can transform you and calm you down when you are overwhelmed.

For years people took smoke breaks to collect themselves. I get it, wanting the space to collect yourself, but breathing in toxic chemicals is not the way to go. That doesn't mean you can't partake in that ritual of pausing, of taking a break, without the chemicals.

It almost sounds too simple. It's not.

Breathing is power.

Breathing is life.

Use it.

Exercise: Breathe. Notice what it feels like to breathe.

Put one hand on your abdomen and breathe deeply, very deeply and slowly, until your hand rises as air travels all the way down into your abdomen. Hold it for a couple of seconds and release it slowly and completely. Expel everything you can. Hold it a second, maybe two, then breathe in again slowly and deeply. Repeat this ten times. Notice how you feel when your blood is fully oxygenated and you take time to focus on simply breathing.

Use your breath as a tool when you are feeling stressed and overwhelmed. If there's not time for ten, take three or four. If there's not time for three or four, take one. Learn to use your breath as a source of calm. When you need a moment to reset and collect yourself, bring your attention to your breath.

THE OTHER SIDE OF FEAR.

The worst part is over. The fear of what you're going through now was likely heavier than where you are. Full disclosure - my marriage should have ended many years before it did. But fear kept me rooted in pain.

I felt so much fear and so much anxiety over what it would be like — how it would hurt, whether or not I could provide for myself and my kids, how my children might suffer, how I might have to sell my house and give up so many material comforts. Even thinking about it now brings up a visceral physical heaviness — I felt that fear through every inch of my body. When I thought about those fears, I felt like I was suffocating beneath them. I couldn't breathe. The fear itself was taking away my breath, my power, and I was paralyzed feeling like there was nothing I could do with the weight of the fear upon me. I couldn't move, much less act.

I was stuck beneath the heaviness of my fear.

That moment when I realized the pain of my marriage was worse than anything I feared was terrifying and also exhilarating. On the one hand, I knew the fear was no longer anchoring me to the weight of my painful dead marriage. And on the other, I was terrified of having to sift through everything I feared.

On the other side of divorce, I learned the fear itself was worse than anything I feared.

The pain, the financial stresses, challenges for my kids, letting go of the house and material comforts — it was nothing compared to the fear that pinned me down for so many years. Letting go of that fear was freeing. It didn't happen all at once. I held on to the house for a long time, and the process of selling it and getting out of it was incredibly challenging but so liberating. I have never felt such great freedom as I felt creating a home in a house that he was never a part of.

Take a gander at all that fear you carried around and maybe some of it that you still do and rest assured, it won't be easy, but the fear is probably far worse than the reality of what lies ahead.

Once you tackle it, it gets easier and easier, and you discover a great truth that I hope you will hold tight throughout this journey:

You are stronger and fiercer than you ever imagined.

Exercise: Debunk your fears.

Create a list of your biggest fears around the loss of your marriage. Then go through each of them and ask yourself, "What's the worst thing that could really happen?" After that, ask the question, "And then what?"

Break down your fears one by one and then ask yourself what's worse - the fear that holds you back or the actual thing you fear?

Here's an example: "I'm afraid of losing my house." Well, if I lose my house, I will have to move. That won't be easy, but I can figure that out. I will scrape together a deposit and find something to rent that is suitable for now. I will find a new home, maybe smaller or less desirable, but I will make it work. And then we will start over in our new home and move on. The fear of losing the house is far more intense than the reality of making your way through it.

BEWARE OF FORMIDABLE ADVERSARIES: DEPRESSION, ANXIETY, PTSD.

When you go through a profound life stressor, you are more prone to mental health issues. It doesn't make you weak. It makes you human.

Depression is a bitch. It's not the same thing as sadness. Depression is different for different people, but common symptoms include tearfulness, feeling foggy headed, difficulty making decisions, inability to enjoy activities that once brought pleasure, lack of interest in previous hobbies, hopelessness, helplessness, and changes in appetite or sleep.

I remember being in couples therapy with a very seasoned couples therapist while I was in the fog of depression. I couldn't think and all I wanted to do was sit on her sofa and cry. She looked at me and then looked at my then husband and said, "Let's work with you today. She's obviously depressed." And she was dead-on because I wasn't truly capable of anything that day other than crying on her couch.

I remember that feeling of being in the right place to do what I needed to do but having no ability to do anything at all because something in me was not right. When I see a client who is genuinely depressed, not merely sad, I often look at them and tell them that I know. It's bad there. It feels like there is no getting out. But there is. I know this because I have seen it in my practice with my clients and also because I have experienced it. You may need help. I did.

Anxiety sometimes comes packaged with depression, but sometimes it's separate and aside or even protects us from sinking into depression. All of the balls are spinning and if we focus on all of the balls and keeping them in the air, we don't have to feel the pain. Symptoms of anxiety include excessive worry or intrusive worrisome thoughts, a feeling of being restless or on edge, feeling easily fatigued, difficulty concentrating, irritability, muscle tension, and sleep issues.

For me, anxiety was at its height when I first threw my ex out years before I divorced him. I felt it was imperative to reach a child development expert (I was not yet a therapist) and immediately researched and called every expert in the field I could find to figure out how to not screw up my daughter. It was not urgent. It felt urgent. Anxiety can be exhausting. You may need help. I did.

PTSD symptoms may come up if you were traumatized in your marriage or in the process of leaving it. Heightened startle response, feeling in danger or threatened, hypervigilance where you feel like you have to constantly be on the lookout, flashbacks, nightmares, and symptoms of anxiety and/or depression are often signs of PTSD. PTSD can also be exhausting. You may need help. I did.

Honestly, that first time I threw my ex out, I suffered pretty intensely from anxiety, depression, and PTSD. It was much less intense when I ended my marriage. I think the reason is that I went to a lot of therapy (individual therapy and group therapy) in between and took a hard look at how I got there and what I wanted for myself moving forward. That therapeutic work cultivated strength and coping skills that I didn't have before as well as insight that left me feeling in a safer place. It was during that time that I pursued my Master's in Clinical Psychology and became a therapist myself.

Medications can help too, although I do think it's best to consult a psychiatrist rather than a general practitioner before going down that route. Your family physician may be quick to prescribe a medication, but it's not in their wheelhouse to understand the nuances of all the different options available. I have taken an

SSRI (an anti-depressant) and I do find that some of my clients who consult a psychiatrist benefit from medication. Currently, I take fish oil, turmeric, and vitamin D daily because there is research to suggest that they are also effective at relieving symptoms of depression.

But I don't credit medication or supplements with my increased ability to manage depression, anxiety, and PTSD. I credit the work I did in therapy — individual, group and even couples which gave me clarity on the context of my relationship (thank you Jenner Bishop, Marnie Breecker, Alexandra Katehakis, and Brenda Beardsley.) I have also had the opportunity ' to help my own clients work through these symptoms and better understand how they got where they are and how they move forward. I strongly believe in the process.

Anxiety, depression, and PTSD impede our ability to connect in a healthy meaningful way to others — from our children to our colleagues to our friends. Often people think they can't afford to get treatment and that it's selfish. I believe the opposite is true. You can't afford not to — it impacts every piece of your life, both personal and professional, when symptoms of anxiety, depression and PTSD take hold. And the people you care about suffer when you don't take care of yourself, not when you do.

Exercise: Evaluate your levels of depression, anxiety, and PTSD.

Take a moment to reflect on your experience with the symptoms I listed in this chapter. Think about what coping skills or activities help alleviate your symptoms. Create a list of those. Go back to this list every time you find yourself struggling.

If you find it's not enough, hop on the *Psychology Today* website and start browsing therapists or get recommendations from friends. Be honest with yourself: how bad is it? Yes, there is pain attached to divorce. However, if you are suffering and it feels helpless and hopeless for a sustained period of time, please reach out for help.

START WITH THE (WO)MAN
IN THE MIRROR.
MAINTAIN YOUR INTEGRITY.

Don't judge yourself for thoughts and feelings that are cruel or ugly. Thoughts and feelings come and go. They do not define who you are. They do not define who you will be. Don't judge yourself harshly if you have thoughts or feelings you don't like. It's your brain processing. Allow yourself to have the thoughts and feelings even if you sometimes feel like a murderous bitch for having them.

It will pass. I promise. I know. I have wished my ex (and the father of my children) dead many, many times, imagined getting on a plane and flying far away where nobody can find me many, many times, thought about telling people in my community the truth about what my ex has done many, many times, about taking my kids to live somewhere quiet and far away from their dad many, many times... the list goes on. I have thoughts that are cruel, stupid, sabotaging, and illegal. But that's okay, because I have never taken any action on any of these thoughts and they always pass. Always.

Action is another story. Actions cannot be undone.

There is nothing wrong with you for having thoughts and feelings that you don't like. But be careful. Don't act on them. I have often wanted that *Waiting to Exhale* moment when Angela Basset, having discovered her husband's lies, lights his car on fire. I have wanted to share everything, tell all, and let him go up in flames. But I don't do it. And the reason has nothing to do with preserving him. It's about preserving me.

Integrity is something I value tremendously. Our integrity is not built on how we feel or what we think — it's about the actions we take. Integrity is the space I hold up with compassion, decency, and honesty that allows me to breathe, knowing that whatever anybody else does or thinks, I am okay with me and the choices I have made. I can be alone with myself without questioning who I am or what I do to others.

I treat my ex with decency, kindness and compassion even if I don't always feel compassionate towards him. I don't engage in nastiness or anything below-the-belt. Have I ever thought about it? Yes!!!! Do I ever want to? Absolutely. But I don't, no matter how strong the thoughts and feelings. Because that's not who I want to be and the actions we choose define us. I tell my closest friends those thoughts but not him. I don't tell him because I rest easier knowing that I have not said or done anything to compromise my integrity, my safe space.

Keep that in mind. You can have a thought or feeling without acting on it. Thoughts and feelings can be confusing or painful, but they are harmless. You are not a bad person for having the thought. Remember that and be conscious of it so that when this divorce is behind you, you can look yourself in the mirror and feel good about who you are.

This doesn't mean you can't process your thoughts or feelings. Choose trusted friends to confide in and let it rip. It's necessary (thank you Maggie, Callie, Janine, Danielle, Erica, Rosetta, Mandy and all the other friends who protect the darkness of some of my thoughts and feelings).

I say all this, and I also understand the value of being able to tell your ex to fuck off. There's room for that too, but you need to be savvy and do it without any blowback on you. The good news is there is a way and I will teach you that in the next chapter.

Exercise: Find your trusted friends.

Create a list of trusted friends who can hold your darkest thoughts and feelings without judgment. This list is important. These people will support you and be there for you through the course of your divorce. When you are tempted to behave in ways that lack integrity, lean on these friends.

If this exercise is hard, I encourage you to try to build friendships. Look for a divorce support group or attend some meet-ups. If you don't have the friends there right now, it's time to go find them. There's even support on-line including my own Facebook support group (You Got This: Healing Through Divorce) — join us there if you'd like. However, online relationships don't take the place of human connection, so seek out friendship close to home too.

THE ART OF THE INVISIBLE 'F' YOU: HOW TO SAY "FUCK YOU" TO YOUR EX WITHOUT HIM EVER KNOWING IT.

One night, during a heated argument via text message with my soon-to-be-ex-husband, I had an epiphany. Arguing with him, trying to persuade him to understand me, was only making things worse for me. The more I tried to reason with him, the more he lashed out at me and the more intense his threats about money and custody became. I was scared and this was escalating. My words fueled his rage and thus only deepened my pain. What I was doing was not working.

He wanted me to tell him I was grateful. He wanted me to thank him for every tiny little thing he did. He wanted me to apologize for snapping at him when he didn't follow through on promises he made. He wanted me to apologize for even having a feeling that he did not like - seeing any sign of anger on my face, even when I didn't even speak words - infuriated him during the process of our divorce.

I did not want to tell him the things he wanted to hear, but I needed to say them to keep things from getting worse than they already were. I had to thank him. I had to tell him I was sorry. I had to placate him. And it was not enough to only say these things. I had to say them convincingly. Saying them felt like a lie, like a contradiction of who I was and what I believed. I felt beaten, intimidated and frightened into saying what he wanted to hear. I didn't like it. It wasn't authentic. I didn't feel empowered.

I felt disgust and sadness. And that's when it came to me —

I had to create a secret language:

Here's my Dictionary:

"Thank you" means *"Fuck you."*
"I am so grateful" means *"You are such an asshole."*
"I am so sorry" means *"You are an idiot."*

For the next several days, I used my language liberally showering him with words of gratitude that only I knew the true meaning of (well, okay, I let a few trustworthy friends in on it too, which gave me people to laugh with). It was empowering and felt amazing. To tell you the truth, it had an interesting effect that I did not expect.

He was so annoyed. "Stop thanking me so much." "You don't have to thank me for everything."

Ha ha ha. I am so sorry. But I am just so incredibly grateful.

I highly recommend creating your own secret language. Find the words that serve you, the ones your soon-to-be former spouse needs to hear to make your life easier and make them mean what feels right to you. It's empowering to be able to routinely tell your husband to go fuck himself without him knowing it. And on some level, he may know it, but he can't accuse you of it, which is an added bonus.

Do not ever tell your ex about your secret language. It might feel like a good idea in some fleeting moment, but do not be tempted. This will ruin it. One of the great gifts in my divorce is being able to smile at my ex-husband and say 'fuck you' any day I feel like it with absolutely zero repercussion.

The Art of the Invisible F You was a source of comfort and joy during my divorce. I hope you are able to enjoy it too.

Exercise: Create your own secret language.

What would you like to say to your ex if you knew there was absolutely no consequence for saying it? What does your ex want to hear from you? Pair up the words he wants to hear from you with the words you'd really like to say and match them up to create your own secret language. Have fun with it. Simple works best.

RUN IN THE RAIN.

There is a sign in the bathroom of my office that says, "Life is not waiting for the storm to pass but learning to dance in the rain." I am a terrible dancer but learning to run in the rain changed my life. Before my divorce, I probably would have been too cautious. Sleeping in the rain is alluring, and what I reluctantly discovered is that running in the rain feels even better. The first time I tried running in the rain, I felt nervous and extremely hesitant. Now I look forward to the rain so that I have the opportunity to run through it.

Running in the rain is liberating. Sleeping in on a rainy day without a husband to cuddle feels sucky. What worked for me before doesn't work for me anymore. I needed to change my life drastically so that it felt rich rather than hollowed.

Look for as many and different opportunities to run in the rain as you can. Challenge yourself to find fulfillment in the activities and choices you've never tried before.

Your running in the rain may not be running at all. It's not about running or dancing or rain, really. It's about bending and stretching who you are, letting go of rigidity, and molding yourself into a new and improved self. Push out of your comfort zone and try something new even when it is not what's easiest. You may be surprised by what happens when you do.

Exercise: Challenge yourself to come up with activities you've never tried before and try them.

What is running in the rain for you? What have you been too scared, too tired, or too rigid to try? Find as many different activities as you can and go try them. See what it feels like. This is an exercise in flexibility and it's an opportunity to discover pieces of yourself that you may not even know exist. Yet.

IF YOU SPRINKLE WHEN YOU TINKLE, BE A SWEETIE, WIPE THE SEATIE.

I found this message scratched into the door of a toilet stall at the mall where I hung out during high school. I remember it to this day. I am sure that whoever scrawled that message into the toilet stall was concerned about keeping the toilet seat dry, but I find it to be a wise adage nonetheless: You don't want to be the asshole who didn't wipe the seat and left a mess for someone unsuspecting who didn't deserve it.

If your anger spills out in ugly ways, clean it up so the rest of the people in your life don't have to deal with it. I don't care how cool and collected you are, you are going to have some moments when you are not. It's healthy, normal and understandable. And you need to take responsibility and own it when it happens.

You have every right to be angry and you may behave badly at times even when you're not trying to. That anger is part of the grieving process. There is nothing wrong with you for feeling it. Let yourself to be as angry as you need to be. Don't hold back. Part of the journey of this book, part of my journey in writing this book, is getting in touch with that anger and protecting yourself, myself, in healthy ways. But at the end of the day, the one who has to live with the choices you make is you. You are human, like me. We do the best we can. It doesn't always feel like enough.

Real life examples: My first Thanksgiving after ending my marriage, I was a wreck. I cooked Thanksgiving dinner by myself while managing children acting out and having no adult company or help. I went into the backyard. I cried and started throwing shit. As far as I knew, I was alone out there and so this seemed perfectly fine and acceptable. It made me feel a little better.

But my then two-year-old daughter snuck into the backyard and saw me. She was confused and started to cry, and I felt horrible. I collected myself and explained that sometimes mommies have big feelings too, and it's okay to feel sad. I made sure she knew that me being sad had nothing to do with anything she had done and that I loved her.

Other examples include easy targets like unwelcome solicitors, telemarketers, bad drivers or unhelpful customer service representatives. It's easy to sprinkle on them. Early on, I had a frustrating issue with my phone that had me practically in tears at the store. I was being ridiculous, but it had nothing to do with the stupid phone. A simple apology is usually enough to wipe the seat in those instances.

It's never intentional but you're going through one of life's greatest all-time stressors. You are going to have moments when you sprinkle. It's okay. There's no permanent damage. Don't beat yourself up.

Just wipe the seat.

Exercise: Reflect on the anger. When have you sprinkled, and did you wipe the seat?

Take a moment to reflect on your anger. When has it spilled over in ways that hurt people who didn't deserve your wrath? Did you clean it up? Is there still time to clean it up? What does your anger look like? What does it feel like? Allow yourself to feel that anger for a heartbeat and have compassion for it — of course you are angry. Of course you are.

Breathe.

You are enough.

Your anger makes sense.

COMPASSION IS THE GENTLEST WAY THROUGH THE CORPSE OF YOUR DEAD MARRIAGE.

The cleanest way through the rancid decaying remains of your marriage is by the light of compassion. Kindness is an easier road. It's hard sometimes but it feels better, and it will actually leave you more motivated and more capable.

I'm not talking about compassion for your ex. I'm talking about compassion for yourself.

There may be things you did in the marriage or choices you made that you regret. People are not perfect. I am not. Even if your marriage was like mine and you had to walk away to protect yourself from painful deception and betrayal, you (I) made choices that landed you (me) there too. And maybe you even lied and betrayed your partner. If you screwed up, that does not make you a screw-up. You deserve compassion too.

If you're like me, you're going to beat up on yourself sometimes for the choices you've made, and I encourage you to back off and do something kind for yourself instead. But ultimately, do you want your kids to beat themselves up for their mistakes? Of course not — but if they see you do it, they will learn to do the same. Treat yourself with as much compassion as you would treat your children. They are watching you.

You did the best you could. Don't be so hard on yourself. Sounds so simple. But this is something I struggle with a lot. Being kind to yourself is more important than you may realize. When you beat yourself up, you feel defeated. When you feel defeated, you are not as capable and you don't feel motivated, which means you accomplish less of what you want and feel more stuck.

Negative self-talk does not help you no matter what you are telling yourself. It holds you back. Finding compassion for yourself empowers you.

Exercise: Challenge the bully (you).

Would you ever let someone talk to you as harshly as you talk to yourself? Probably not, right?

Identify the cruel and damaging self-talk you beat yourself up with. Now imagine what you would say to someone if they spoke that way to you. Stand up for yourself. Hear that voice.

Next, if you heard those bullying words spoken to your child, what would you say to your child? Hear that voice.

That bullying voice inside you is one of many. You may not always be able to get that bully to disappear, but you can make the other voices louder. Connect with those compassionate voices. When you hear the bully, stand up for yourself and nurture yourself with kind, more positive self-talk. Don't let the bully keep you down.

Empower yourself with compassion.

IT DOESN'T MATTER IF HE UNDERSTANDS YOU. RELAX AND ASSUME THAT HE/SHE NEVER WILL.

For years, I wanted my husband to empathize with me. I wanted him to understand where I was coming from, but the conversation always returned to him. He couldn't help it. I wanted an emotionally intimate marriage, so I continued to try.

The marriage was over, and it does not matter if he has empathy or compassion for me. I am done trying to squeeze wine out of a stone. It's a huge relief to not feel the frustration and disappointment of him not understanding. But now I have to sit with the discomfort of knowing that he has absolutely no clue where I am coming from when before, I had some shadow of hope that maybe I had helped him understand.

It doesn't matter if he understands you. You gave up on the marriage. You gave up on him. Accepting that he likely doesn't understand and never will makes the road ahead so much easier.

This issue came up for me often with emails. He'd send an email saying things that were absurd and my knee-jerk was to respond and explain to him how misguided he was as though maybe I could help him to understand. Most often, it was a waste of time and energy and made things worse. When I stopped responding to all of the stupid stuff he wrote in his emails and stopped caring about what he thought of me, I got my time and energy back. The stuff he made up about what was happening was completely off-base but I no longer felt any need to correct it. It doesn't matter.

And after a while, since I didn't respond to it, he stopped sending it. Any feedback, positive or negative, is feedback. By engaging with him at all, I was encouraging him unconsciously to continue doing it. When I stopped caring if he understood me and I stopped responding, he stopped sending me nonsense. If you're sick of his stupid emails or texts, my suggestion is simple: stop responding to it.

There is one exception that I learned from a wonderful book called *Splitting* by Bill Eddy. If your ex emails you something that is factually incorrect and requires correction for legal purposes, you may need to correct him in a very calm and unemotional way with as few words as possible. The reason for this is that if he makes accusations that are factually untrue and you do not respond and the emails are admitted into court record, your lack of response may look like an admission of guilt. This is very tricky, but if you get an email with accusations that might make you look bad in court, consider responding with only a correction of the factual information and no emotional engagement whatsoever. This is also liberating because his crazy email is met with your very rational, calm, factual correction. If anybody ever reads it, they will see his craziness.

> ### *Exercise: Create a system for emails and texts.*
>
> Set up a file or email folder on your computer where you put any emails or texts that your ex sends to you which are inflammatory or inappropriate. You may need them for legal purposes one day.
>
> The next time you get an incendiary email or text from your ex, put it in your email folder and then ask yourself this question: does it require a response? If there is no factual information that needs to be corrected for legal purposes or the safety of your children, do not respond at all. If there is, write a response with no emotion simply correcting any information that requires correction or response. Send a blind copy (BCC) to yourself and save that in your file too.

IF YOU KEEP THINKING ABOUT YOUR EX AND IT HURTS...

Over and over again, I hear women in my 'You Got This: Healing Through Divorce' group on Facebook talk about how they wake up thinking about their ex and want to stop.

This is what you need to do: Think badly of him.

It is rare that I recommend negative thinking, but this is an exception. Our thoughts inform our feelings which inform our behavior and also our thoughts. If you are thinking about happy times with your ex, you will feel sad and miss them. You may even send an email or text that you will later regret. So stop it. Don't think about the good stuff. This is not the time.

Try this instead: Think about the worst moments of your relationship. Remember all of the unkind things your ex did and how hurt you felt. Go over your decision to divorce and remind yourself of why you made that decision. Then remind yourself of the things you like about yourself and why you are worth more. Focus on your love for yourself. You are likely to feel more empowered. And when you feel empowered, you are more likely to do something empowering and thus think empowered thoughts.

If you have a pattern of waking up missing your ex, change it with this simple strategy. I know it's easier said than done. But you can change the way you think if you are mindful about it.

Exercise: Create a list of dislikes.

Create a list of all of the things you dislike about your ex, all of the unkind things they did in your marriage, and all of the ways in which they let you down. Don't hold back here. Remember why you chose to pursue a divorce and write it down on this list along with all of the little annoying things your ex did when you were married. Make this list as exhaustive as possible.

Also create a list of things you love about yourself and why you are worthy of better than how your ex treated you.

Keep these lists handy so that anytime you find yourself missing your ex, you can refer back to them.

LISTEN TO YOUR BODY.

Listen to and treat your body with the utmost respect. You take it for granted but it's taking a beating too.

People think that psychosomatic means crazy. It does not. Your central nervous system runs through every inch of your body, so the pain and trauma of your divorce is likely to bring actual physical pain too. Be gentle and treat your body with kindness. But there is more.

Pay attention to what your body is telling you. Notice how it feels and what it needs from you. When I gave birth to my twins, labor came on suddenly and quickly. When I arrived at the hospital, the nurse examined me and said that I was only dilated to 3. She went away to chat with the nurses. Within ten minutes, I was in intense pain and I told my then-husband to go get the nurse because I had to push. He did so and he came back and explained to me, laughing impishly, that the nurses said not to push. But I knew. My body had to push. I told him to go back there and tell her to come in immediately. He resisted but ultimately agreed and the reluctant nurse returned with an eye roll. When she examined me, her face went pale and her jaw dropped. I was at 10 plus 2 meaning the first of my twins was on his way out. My nurse apologized profusely and explained that I was having a precipitous delivery and she had never seen anyone progress this fast before. Suddenly, my room was flooded with doctors and nurses and I was wheeled into the operating room. I knew my body. I don't know what would have happened if I had not spoken up.

I remind myself of this story sometimes because I tend to disconnect from my body and deny my experience of it, often convincing myself that I am wrong, and I am fine when I am not. That is the wrong thing to do. Noticing the experience of your body, heeding it, is critical. The stress of divorce takes a toll. Without your living, breathing body, you have nothing.

Someone close to me began having gastrointestinal symptoms immediately following her divorce. She paid attention, sought help and got the appropriate tests. As a result, she caught a rare malignant tumor in her pancreas early enough and is doing well. I'm not telling you divorce causes cancer. What I am saying is that it is critical to pay attention to your body during this painful process because if you disconnect from your physical experience, you may not take proper care of yourself and inadvertently make this difficult time even harder.

Think about the way you eat and how you treat your body. I changed the way I ate when I threw my ex out because I became more conscious and connected to how food made me feel. I encourage you to do the same. Notice how you feel when you eat certain foods. I made surprising discoveries and my diet doesn't resemble what I ate before my split. My body doesn't either. I feel much better.

Soothing with sugar may feel good in the moment, but check-in with how you feel afterward. How strong, how calm, how motivated are you? Numbing out with sugar doesn't feel good for long and turning to sugar can become addictive. Be mindful of how you use food. It can be used to fuel you and make you feel strong, but if you use it to escape, it can derail you.

If it's derailed you already, it's not too late to get back on track. Not tomorrow, not next week or next month or this summer — right now, in this moment. Focus less on deprivation and more on how you fuel yourself. If this feels impossible, consider getting help to untangle your relationship with food. *Intuitive Eating* by Evelyn Tribole is a fantastic resource to examine your relationship with food.

Pamper your body. Treat it like the sacred gift that it is. Remember, the central nervous system runs through every inch of your body. That applies to stress, but it applies to the good stuff too. Taking care of your body has a positive impact psychologically and a big impact on mood. A decadent lotion or a warm bath may soothe your body and soothe your soul. And our bodies are also soothed by touch, so consider getting a massage or pedicure.

Yoga is another gentle treat that is healthy self-care for your body. My clients who resist yoga the most are the ones who tend to get the most out of it if they keep with it. Yoga encourages flexibility both in body and spirit. People who struggle with rigidity don't like it, but they need it more than they realize.

Make a genuine effort to take care of your body in a way that feels meaningful to you.

Exercise: Consider your relationship with your body.

Take a moment to scan your body starting at the top of your head and working your way downward. Notice what you feel in your body. Take stock of your physical self and how you are doing on a physical level.

Next, take some time to consider how you take care of your physical body. When was the last time you had a physical? Is it time? Are there appointments you have been putting off?

Finally, how can you pamper your body? Make a plan to do something that feels soothing and like healthy self-care for you.

EULOGIZE YOUR MARRIAGE. EMPHASIZE GRATITUDE.

If this sounds impossible right now, don't do it. Wait until it doesn't feel so heavy. I am not always in a place to be able to see gratitude for my marriage. In fact, I am usually not in a place to see gratitude for my marriage. However, I believe that there is meaning in everything and to not be able to find any gratitude in this journey that is coming to an end makes the loss too great.

Here's mine:

Dear dead marriage,

I am grateful for the three beautiful children you gave me. They are amazing.

I am grateful for the lessons I have learned from you, however painful some of them may have been to endure. I learned that my ability to manage people is not always a good thing and that I need to pay closer attention to that in my life moving forward. I learned that I am stronger, fiercer, and more independent than I ever imagined. I learned what I want and what I don't want from a life partner. I learned that having a life partner does not complete me and in fact, having the life partner that I did actually depleted me. I learned that I am flawed and my judgment is not always the best, but I have also learned to see my shortcomings and have an awareness of them. I am grateful for the friendships that I have forged during and after my marriage and all of the support that I have found as a result of the pain I have endured. I am grateful to know through this journey that I have amazing friends who will be there for me when I need them.

I am grateful for the gifts my ex-husband did give me — I don't mean the material ones. He supported me, and while his actions were not always kind, he was often kind to me. I am grateful for the adventures I did enjoy with him. I am grateful for the growth his bad behavior sparked in me. It was the worst of him that inspired me to shift careers and get a Master's in Clinical Psychology. I am grateful that his struggles spurred me to grow and opened the door to a new career for me.

The worst in him forced me to find the best in me. I am genuinely grateful for that.

Exercise: Write your eulogy.

In what ways did your marriage shape who you've become? What were its gifts? Why was your marriage a part of the journey? Find the meaning in your marriage. How did it ignite your growth and what gifts did you walk away with?

OLD WOUNDS SURFACE.
GRIEVING LOSSES.

Don't be surprised if this divorce unearths other losses. It did for me. I miss my daddy — for real. It's confusing to feel an old wound so acutely when, at first glance, it feels so unrelated to the pain of divorce.

One morning, on a run, I started crying and didn't know why. This happens sometimes. Just when I think I am on fire and doing great, I get steamrolled by feelings that I can't get a handle on. But on this particular morning, I felt out of my skin. I ran and I cried and ran and cried. I must have looked like a crazy person, but I didn't care. After a little while, I realized that it was the anniversary of my father's death and once I put that together, I bawled like a baby.

On more than one occasion, I have found myself really missing my dad. He died when I was sixteen and has been gone for a long time now. But I could really use a dad right now. I want someone to give me a hug, sit me down and say, "Look, kiddo, this is what you need to do." I want someone to take care of me, but I am at a point in my life where nobody takes care of me but me and I am taking care of everyone. It's not easy.

This divorce brings that up in a profound way. I trusted my husband to take care of me for fifteen years. He failed me, but at least there was an illusion that someone was there. And now nobody is there. But me. And I feel that little girl aching for her daddy to come take care of her.

I don't know what your losses are, but don't be surprised if they rise to the surface and ache a little bit more than they usually do during this time. It's painful. You may find yourself crying like a baby for a loss that you suffered years or even decades ago.

There is something about divorce that leaves us naked and raw with salt spilling over open wounds. You're not alone. It is hard. Allow yourself to feel the pain and remember, it will pass. It always does.

Exercise: Assess your wounds.

How has this divorce touched your old wounds? Has your divorce unearthed anything painful? Take a moment to reflect on any wounds that feel raw right now. It's okay to feel it. If that feels scary, ask yourself why. What will happen if you allow yourself to feel that pain or sadness? Being mindful of those old wounds may help you heal. Again, be compassionate with yourself.

IT FEELS LIKE THE WORLD MAY END BUT YOU'RE OKAY.

This is a random story but it's one I think of often that resonates for me. Years ago, I was in a hotel with my three children and my then-husband. This hotel chain offers a unique strategy for energy efficiency — you must dock your key at the power source. If you remove your key, all of the power goes out.

One day, I am in this hotel room in the bathroom where there are no windows and no natural light, and my then-husband decides to get something out of the car. My oldest daughter is sleeping in one of the beds, so I am quietly attempting to give a bath to my then-two-year-old twins in the bathroom with the door closed. My ex (who was officially my ex about two months later), without thinking about it, takes the key out of the power source and walks out. Moments later —

I am in a pitch-dark bathroom (no windows so no light whatsoever) with two screaming two-year-olds and I cannot see a thing. Even worse, the light switch does nothing because the light switches don't work when the key is removed. Upon hearing my twins scream, my older daughter woke up screaming too. I couldn't even find the knob on the door because it was so damn dark. I couldn't soothe my babies because I couldn't see them. I was horrified. In that moment, as strange as it may sound, I felt like I might die. It felt like they might die, drown in that tub, which was even worse. In that moment, the world was about to end. I was having a trauma response and my children were too. I was terrified.

What's important about this story is that you know as well as I do that I did not die. In fact, we were all fine after about five terrifying and upsetting minutes in our lives and a great deal of screaming and discomfort which left us all in a horrible mood for all of about a half hour.

It felt like we would not survive it as it was happening. Left alone in the dark by myself with my screaming children was horrifying. And yet we did survive it.

You may feel alone in the dark right now and it may feel like the world will end. It won't.

That moment in the dark in the bathroom, that's what divorce is like in the beginning. You can't see anything and it feels like you all might die. To make matters worse, everyone tells you how sorry they are when they hear the news, as though you are already dead.

You are not dead. You will not die from this. The journey may not be easy. It may hurt like hell. But you will look back at these five minutes of your life as a blip one day.

Remember the English proverb: "Just when the caterpillar thought the world was over, it became a beautiful butterfly." Even the lights in the hotel will come back on.

Exercise: When have you experienced your darkest moments? Did you survive?

Take a moment to reflect on your darkest moments when you felt that you might not make it through. If you're there right now, this is not the moment to reflect on. Think back to another time that felt dark and hopeless when you thought you would never survive. Did you survive? Of course, I know the answer to that and so do you. But in the darkest moments, remind yourself that it's not the first time you thought the world would end. Remember that because when it's dark in there, it's easy to forget that the light will come back on.

THE BEAUTY OF AN ELOQUENT 'FUCK YOU' LETTER.

There are two rules with an effective 'fuck you' letter. Only two, but they are critical. Any deviation from either of these rules ruins it.

The first rule: Do not hold back. Do not protect him. Do not caretake for him or go out of your way to try to understand where he is coming from. Caretaking is when we think about how other people feel and take care of their needs ahead of our own and sometimes to our own detriment. Caretaking of his feelings is worthless right now. Don't bother. It is only an impediment to your own healing.

Do not be kind or gentle when writing your letter. Let yourself be angry. Put that anger in your letter. I am not telling you that you can't have empathy for your ex. But that's not what this letter is about. This letter is about moving through anger and to do that, you've got to let yourself feel the anger. Many women are taught to hide their anger and that their anger is not acceptable, but anger is a healthy, normal emotion.

Allowing yourself to feel it is important. Go ahead, get angry. You have plenty of reason to.

Berate him for how he disappointed you, how he hurt you, how he continues to hurt you. It doesn't have to be articulate or well-written and if some of what you have to say is raw and unfair, that's fine. Nothing is uncalled for in your 'fuck you' letter. You can write whatever you want. You can use cruel language if that feels good or you can take the high road and patronize him. Either way. You can write whatever you want. But you have to write it. You can go back and write more, but don't hold back. This letter is for you. Nobody else is going to see it.

And here's the other rule. DO NOT BREAK THIS RULE. It is the most important one:

YOU MAY NOT SEND THIS LETTER TO HIM EVER!

Hide the stamps before you write it.

Do not be tempted to write it in email or text form.

No matter how brilliant you believe it to be, no matter how much he needs to hear what you've said, no matter how much wine you've had to drink, **DO NOT SEND IT**.

If you send it, it will make your life more difficult. It will make your children's lives more difficult. It can even be used against you in a court of law if you actually give it to your ex. No good can come from giving him the letter.

This letter is about you. For you. Your husband doesn't deserve it. If it feels meaningful to you to burn it (safely, of course), then do it. Don't give it to him.

Another word of warning - your children should never read this either, so make sure you put it somewhere safe where they will never come across it. No good can come from them reading this letter.

Exercise: Write your 'fuck you' letter.

Do it for you. Keep it for you. Do not hold back. Your anger is worthwhile. This letter is a safe place for it. I considered putting my own fuck you letter in this book, but then realized I would be breaking my own rule by doing so — my kids could come across it. But rest assured, I have written more than one of these letters myself, and it feels good.

CONSIDER A FREEDOM RING.

After I let go of my marriage and stopped wearing my wedding ring, my hand felt bare. An amazing friend of mine (thanks, Danielle) who had gone through a divorce told me that she sold her ring and used the money to buy a piece of jewelry she loved. She called it her 'freedom ring'. She did remarry. She is happy in her new marriage. And she still wears her freedom ring. It's a symbol of her reclaiming herself and I love it. Letting go of the ring that shackled you in your broken marriage doesn't mean your hands have to be bare.

I sold my ring but did not feel comfortable buying an expensive ring to be my freedom ring. I couldn't afford it. I bought an inexpensive ring — the stone is sea glass which feels meaningful to me. The ocean brings me comfort — it's my favorite place to run and find peace, it's my children's favorite place to play, and it's where my father's ashes are scattered. It cost me less than $100 and I love my freedom ring and everything it represents. My hand no longer feels bare.

Money may be tight, but you don't have to spend a fortune to do this. Treat yourself if you can to a freedom ring and remind yourself that your freedom is worth so much more than any diamond you once wore.

Exercise: Think about your freedom ring. Start shopping.

You don't have to buy it right away but start to think about your freedom ring and what you want it to look like. If it's fun for you, window shop or browse. Don't make purchases you cannot afford but allow yourself the fun and healthy distraction of shopping for your freedom ring.

SAY HI TO YOUR HIGHER POWER. CONNECTING TO SPIRITUALITY.

Whether it's God, Buddha, Jesus, SpongeBob Squarepants or nature and the universe itself, connect to your higher power in a way that feels meaningful to you. It really doesn't matter what you call it if it feels spiritual to you.

For me, connecting to my higher power is connecting with nature and appreciating the sanctity of the world we live in. Meditation, yoga, walks and deep breathing feel like meaningful ways to connect spiritually for me.

If your religion brings you comfort and is the source of your higher power, visit your church or connect to your religious beliefs in a way that feels significant to you.

Spirituality can look so different for different people with differing beliefs. Regardless of your beliefs, bring spirituality into your healing practice without judgment.

Whatever feels meaningful to you is meaningful enough.

Exercise: How does spirituality fortify your journey? What does spirituality mean to you?

Reflect on what your spirituality means to you. If you don't subscribe to religious beliefs, don't dismiss spirituality. Spirituality may connect to religion, but it doesn't have to. Reconnect to your spiritual side — it's in there somewhere and you might find it more comforting than you've imagined. If you don't know what it looks like, try out a meditation app on your phone or pick up a book that catches your attention. Spirituality is often a work in progress.

IT'S OKAY TO FEEL COMPASSION FOR HIM, BUT DON'T TAKE OFF THE SAFETY BAR.

I have to confess, I felt some guilt after writing my 'fuck you' letter when a couple days later my soon-to-be-ex-husband was exceptionally kind and helpful. I felt some guilt when I saw a glimmer of the man I married. I felt some guilt when I remembered that he is not always difficult.

If you have this experience or if you notice moments when you do feel a sense of love for him, hold on to them for the sake of your kiddos. That doesn't mean you should try to work things out - that's a totally different subject. For me, I know my marriage is over and irreparably damaged. There's no going back. Ever. Being able to see his positive qualities and have compassion for him is kind to our children. Being able to connect to the piece that shows up as their father is a good thing. Those moments when I remember he is more than just the asshole I divorced are a gift. And yet these moments can never erase bad behavior or the reasons I have for letting go of this marriage.

Don't beat yourself up with guilt. You didn't send that 'fuck you' letter. Having those thoughts and feelings did not injure your ex or children in any way. In fact, writing that letter and getting it all down might have been a kindness to your ex. Honestly, I think maybe I am better able to feel compassion for my ex and see his kindness because I wrote my tirade down and let it go. I don't see these words and feel the rage as much when I look at him. I am not holding it all back anymore.

But all this being said, don't forget that you're not safe. If he is being kind, be careful. Just as you experience a roller coaster of emotions, so does he. You don't know what's around the next bend. This is a roller coaster out of hell. If you chose divorce, especially if you have kids, there was something about your marriage that was intolerable.

The roller coaster is not over.

Feel compassion. That's okay. Good, even. Compassion is a sign that you are a heart-centered healthy human being.

But do not take off the safety bar. That compassion you feel does not erase where you've been or indicate that he is going to change his ways and treat you kindly moving forward (regardless of whether or not this has been true as of this point). Proceed cautiously and don't mistake compassion for anything more than it is.

Exercise: Connect with compassion.

In what ways do you have compassion for your ex? Take a moment to imagine his journey and this divorce through his eyes — what he is going through. Take a glimpse and then return to yourself. Remind yourself of your journey and the compassion you have for yourself. Acknowledge the compassion you have for him, but don't let it change the boundaries you set to keep yourself safe or the compassion you have for yourself. Compassion is meaningful, important even. But you come first. Don't forget that.

MONEY, MONEY, MONEY, MONEY…

Divorce takes all of your fears about money and lights them up like glow-in-the-dark landmines of terror.

How will you pay the bills? What happens when support steps down? How are you supposed to support your family with so much less? How will you make ends meet or create a sustainable income for yourself while still taking care of your children the way you always have? How will you afford all of the things your children have come to expect when you are taking financial hits?

There will be moments when these questions may feel daunting, overwhelming and nightmarish. I know. I have been there. And here's what I have learned:

Fixating on the fear and allowing it to paralyze you does not help you. You will have to be creative and inventive to navigate issues of money and finances now that you are divorced.

Honestly, eating out still brings me intense anxiety as it triggers all of my fears around money and finances. I can't buy a $10 lunch without thinking that I can't afford it, that I shouldn't splurge like this. It's silly at times. I can't make the fear go away but I can remind myself that I will get through it. I will figure it out. And I will. And I am.

There are easy simple things that you can do to navigate financial challenges, especially in the early days when you may be feeling more of a financial crunch. One of the first things I did was change my eating habits. I began to eat more simply and cost-effectively. Eggs are a fantastic and inexpensive meal. Nuts go a long way. Fruits and vegetables are also relatively inexpensive and can be eaten raw, saving time as well. Eating at home is a huge cost-cutter, especially if you can enjoy simple healthy foods.

Cutting back on non-essential spending helps when you're feeling the financial stress of a divorce. Don't go to Target unless you hold yourself to a strict shopping list. So much cute stuff. If you are in a financial pinch, you don't need it. Not right now. If there was a product at Target that decreased your financial stress, imagine that's what you're checking out with and step away from the shiny pretty objects.

If you can't pay the bills until you settle the divorce issues (like selling property or dividing bank accounts), consider manipulating your credit without damaging it. I was able to maneuver credit card balances using credit card transfers, allowing myself a period of grace with no finance charges or penalties. There was a fee for the credit transfer, but it was far less than the finance charges I would have been saddled with had I blindly decided to live on credit. I also opened new credit cards with 0% apr for one year to get me by, and I paid the minimum balance on those cards until the house was sold and I could afford to get out of my debt.

Some of you may have been reliant on your ex to manage finances for a long time. You are perfectly capable even if it scares you. There is no shame in asking for help. Make sure that you know exactly where your money is and what accounts you have. Pay attention to the balances and if you can, set alerts so that you know if there's any unusual activity. Be clear on what bills get paid how. Set up automatic minimum payments as much as possible as it may save you time and missed payments.

Make sure that you and your ex are clear about how you're handling money and be transparent as you move forward untangling finances. As soon as you can, try to establish separate bank accounts so that you have a safe place for your money that he cannot access. You don't want to drain your joint accounts or suddenly discover that he has — it will only make things worse. Consult an attorney or tax accountant if you have questions about what your financial picture will look like post-divorce and start to think within those limits.

Additionally, there are financial planners who specialize in divorce. Do some research and find one in your area. It might help you navigate your finances.

Another resource is the engagement ring. I sold mine on a website called IdonowIdont.com. It required patience and took some time, but I unloaded it and got a big check. Jewelry shops that sell estate jewelry on consignment are also an option. Be careful not to get scammed.

You will get through this time with more financial savviness and independence than you ever imagined possible. Instead of sitting in the fear, fuel yourself with the passion and excitement that comes with knowing that you will find your way through it.

And then do just that. Find your way through it. It may feel impossible at times, but you will do it.

Exercise: Review your finances. Create a budget.

Take some time to really look at your finances. Where is your money? How much is there? Where are your accounts? What bills do you have? How much money are you bringing in? Are you spending more than you make?

If cash flow is a problem, create a list of things that you can trim your spending on. Look at your credit card bills — where is your money going? Is it Starbucks or Target or lunches out? Think hard about whether or not those expenditures are worth it right now. Consider staying away from those money drains for a while.

Create a budget using an app or a spreadsheet or paper and pencil. Work hard to make it a budget that you can make work for now and try to spend within it.

IT'S OKAY TO HATE HIM SOMETIMES. JUST DON'T KILL HIM.

If you wish he were dead sometimes, you are normal.

When I talk to someone who is struggling in or ending a marriage and I tell them that they are not a bad person for wishing he was dead, they often cry or sigh huge relief or even laugh. Of course you wish he was dead! Divorce sucks. Dealing with the end of the marriage plus having to deal indefinitely with this person you want to be rid of to settle this divorce, or ongoing because of the children you have together? It's awful. Of course, there are moments when a reality without him in it feels like a dream. And of course you know it wouldn't be. You want him to be happy, your kids deserve a father, blah, blah, blah.

There's nothing wrong with you for hating him sometimes. It's perfectly understandable.

Just don't kill him.

SOMETIMES YOU JUST HAVE TO HOLD THE SHIT IN YOUR HAND AND SMILE.

I don't know why life happens this way, but sometimes when bad stuff happens, everything falls apart. Could be an issue of perspective - you see the bad when you feel bad — but it feels more complicated to me than that. My father died when I was a teenager. Of cancer. A month later, my mother was diagnosed with - you guessed it - cancer.

Those next couple of years, I was in the room with two people for the moment they died of cancer (only one was my parent) and saw a lot of pain. I survived it.

Eventually, the storm ended, and life continued with a normal smattering of obstacles rather than the hurricane it had been. But the year my marriage came completely unglued, it felt like everything fell apart again.

Here are some highlights:

My two-year-old son created a flood in the bathroom of my home that spread through the walls and under the wood floors in adjoining rooms in less than two hours. (I believed he was napping, turns out he was playing in my sink). It caused over $20k worth of damage to our home and forced us to move out while repairs to prevent mold damage were completed.

My ex lost two different jobs within a single year, making moving forward with divorce proceedings extremely challenging, and leaving me in a precarious financial position to make ends meet.

My two-year-old daughter fell on her face and split her tooth vertically up the middle. The other half of her tooth had to be removed leaving her without one of her two front teeth for several years. Of course, the dental bill was not cheap.

My nine-year-old daughter fell off her skateboard and severely sprained her ankle.

One of my children started refusing to poop for periods lasting over a week which caused a blockage and necessitated a special diet and regular visits with a GI doctor.

Our dog went for a routine exam and came home with a newly diagnosed heart condition and cancer diagnosis which required expensive surgeries and procedures. The vet bill was not pretty.

My computer died. The Genius Bar stamped a time of death. It was toast.

The oven broke and cost hundreds of dollars to repair.

One afternoon, during another of my two-year-old son's naps in my bed, I came in to discover him smiling widely while holding a fistful of poop that he had smeared into my brand-new bedding. That image of him in my bed exemplifies what my life was like during this period. Sometimes you just have to hold the shit in your hands and smile. There won't always be so much of it. But don't be surprised if you are smelling it all around.

Exercise: What's your hurricane? How are you surviving?

Journal on the obstacles you've faced and take a moment to appreciate how much you have overcome already. It's not easy. And yet you're doing it. Try to have a sense of humor about some of it if you can — sometimes when shit hits the fan, it's so ridiculous it's funny.

ENJOY UNEXPECTED SILVER LININGS.

Don't worry. This is not a 'look at the bright side' lecture.

Even when life is hard, there are gifts. Try to find them and enjoy them if you can. For example, the damage my son caused was covered by insurance. All we had to pay was a deductible (which was a lot but could have been worse). And while the week out of our home was exhausting for me, we basically got an all-expense-paid vacation at a hotel on the beach out of what my son did. We lucked into an ocean front room. The weather gods aligned, and the weather was gorgeous in November. We spent every day at the beach playing. I have a series of photographs hanging in my house of that week as a reminder of what an amazing time we had.

Just because some of your life sucks right now doesn't mean it all has to.

It is okay to be angry and overwhelmed and feel love and joy and gratitude too.

Exercise: Connect with gratitude.

What are you grateful for today? If you can, challenge yourself to write down three gratitudes every day. Research shows that making space for gratitude actually increases people's experience of being happy. Find a notebook, make it a gratitude journal, and write down your gratitudes every day. Or get a jar and scribble gratitudes on scraps of paper, then watch the jar fill up. Find a way to work gratitude into your daily routine.

LOOK FOR PLAN B.
AND THEN PLAN C.
AND PLAN D.

All of the stuff that you have and the way your life works — it will change. There were junctures through my divorce where I didn't know what my life would look like from one month to the next. I was terrified of letting go of my 'normal' but the plan I had for my life wasn't possible anymore.

You don't want to sell your house. Okay. But what if you did? Where would you go? What would that actually look like? Imagine it. Think it through. That's your Plan B. For every point that you don't want to consider, contemplate what it would look like if you did it.

Keep doing this. Over and over. Challenge all of the boxes that keep you where you are. Closely examine the pieces that aren't working — if you can't afford your current living situation, your job isn't conducive financially or otherwise to being a single parent, you don't have the support you need or want. Examine those pieces and look at the alternatives that you have never wanted to look at. Looking at them does not mean that you will move forward with them. But sometimes, the options that we think would never work for us turn out to be better than we imagined when we really think them through. And sometimes, we don't have the luxury of not considering other options.

Having a Plan B and Plan C and Plan D helped me feel like I could handle whatever was on the horizon. I did have to move outside of my comfort zone, and having those options thought out ahead of time made it easier for me. There was a time when selling my house and moving didn't seem like an option I would consider. But I had to look more deeply at that option and eventually, I did leave that house. It was the right thing for me.

Another piece to look at are the negative beliefs we have about ourselves that keep us chained to the crashing train. Whenever I hear a client say, "I can't do that. I'm not (fill in the blank) enough," I challenge them. It's true. If you tell yourself you can't, you can't. You will make that so. But changing the story you tell yourself changes the possibilities. When you hear that 'I can't' story and replace it consciously with a story of 'I can,' it suddenly becomes a possibility.

Of course, this sounds simpler than it is. Often those negative stories we tell ourselves are based on negative core beliefs that evolve out of trauma and are reinforced by trauma. That's how our brains work. When something bad happens, we try to make sense of it, and we create a negative belief about ourselves to explain it. Often, these are beliefs like "I am not good enough," "I don't deserve good things," "I am not capable," "I cannot stand up for myself," "I am not safe." The list of unhealthy negative cognitions can fill many pages.

If you are noticing that changing the story you tell yourself isn't working, it may be that unresolved trauma has that negative cognition locked in tight. Therapy can help with that. Eye movement desensitization and reprocessing (EMDR) is a treatment for trauma that specifically examines those negative cognitions and has many years of research to back up its efficacy. If you are feeling stuck with that negative belief, consider looking for a therapist trained in EMDR or other methods of helping you let go of unhealthy cognitions that are keeping you anchored in pain.

To get through this, you may have to consider options that aren't ideal so that you don't get stuck with an outcome that you don't like. Don't put your head in the sand. Consider other options before your options diminish.

I realize that not everybody has the luxury of options like selling the house and some people may be in a more dire place than I was. If resources are thin and you don't have the support you need, look in your community to find out what options exist for you. You can dial 2-1-1 and someone will help you get in touch with local resources if you are destitute and need them.

Exercise: What is your Plan B? Plan C? Plan D?

First, take the time to identify alternative plans and sit with them. What would it look like? Worst case scenario? Best case scenario?

Next, are there any negative stories you're telling yourself about these options? Are there any negative beliefs about yourself holding you back? If there are, change the story. When you notice that unhealthy story coming up, remember the story you want to be telling yourself instead and make the choice to change it.

IT'S JUST STUFF.

The house, the belongings inside it, the cars - try to remember how little that stuff matters. Don't get mired in it. I struggle with this myself. I couldn't imagine losing my home but then when I really thought about it, I couldn't imagine keeping it either. The stuff is not what matters. You will never look back and wish you had more stuff. Don't let worrying about the stuff in your life get in the way of you being able to enjoy the people in it.

Focus on the present.

Collect and enjoy moments and experiences with your friends and your family. Forget the stuff. It will never matter.

If you are struggling and trying to figure out how to pay for basic necessities, consider what those basic necessities are for you. Chasing stuff sometimes keeps us from focusing on what's really important.

Exercise: Reflect on your stuff.

I am a big fan of Marie Kondo's approach to decluttering and minimalism. I believe in that question, "Does it spark joy?" Look at the stuff in your life that "makes you happy". Does it really make you happy, or is that just something you tell yourself? What would life be like without that stuff — would it be that different?

LET GO OF CONTROL.

This is so hard. I'm working on this every day in new and unexpected iterations. Sometimes, it doesn't go down the way you want it to.

I wanted to wait until my daughter finished fifth grade to sell my house and move because we lived three houses down from her elementary school at the time. I had to sell it during the holiday season in the middle of that school year instead. On the ride to school for the rest of that year, my daughter had to watch the new owners build a pool in our old backyard (which she could also see from the playground at her school).

My ex's behavior at softball games impacted my child negatively and there was nothing I could do stop it. My ex lost job after job during the process of our divorce and his salary, thus my support, plummeted — all totally out of my control.

It's not going to always work out the way you want it to no matter how tightly you hold on to the strings.

So let go.

Relax into it.

Even if you can't control it and it doesn't happen as you want it to, you will be okay.

You don't have to control it to be okay.

Exercise: Let go of control.

What do you so desperately want to control right now that you can't? What will happen, truthfully, if you can't control it? Will you survive it? Relax and let go. This is not the same as giving up. The efforts to control the pieces that you can't distract you from the taking charge of the pieces that you can.

What can you let go of?

What do you need to let go of?

What will it mean for you when you do?

DODGING SHITSTORMS.

In the beginning, my ex would create massive drama and I would get sucked into it. He often felt victimized and went on a tirade during which I received page long texts about how unfair and unreasonable I was. Oddly, I could say and do nothing, and he could find reason to fault me. Before long, he began threatening me in his texts about finances and custody. My anxiety would increase with his threats. I would feel a sense of impending doom after our interactions. I did this a lot. Sometimes I even made it worse by engaging with him and replying to his emails or texts with rational messages intended to calm him down but that had exactly the opposite effect.

His shitstorm doesn't have to be yours.

I wonder if I could have understood this advice had someone shared it with me early on, or if I had to learn this lesson myself. I honestly don't know. And you may not be fully able to get this without engaging in some shitstorms of your own. But if you can hear this and understand this, I promise it will make your life easier. I repeat:

His shitstorm doesn't have to be yours.

He can make threats and his world can unravel and if he is feeling intense anxiety, he is almost certain to try to put some of that on you. But you don't have to take it on. You can dodge his shitstorm.

When my ex sent me an email alerting me to his intention to withdraw from mediation, I am sure he thought it would upset me, and it did. For a little while. And then something happened.

I realized that I did not have to respond. I did not have to react. I did not have to do much of anything right then. And I didn't. And I was okay. My kids were okay. I didn't have to engage. Not right then. And eventually, it dissipated. The storm passed. He didn't even follow through on his threat.

Your ex can be a hot mess and you can see it without getting entangled in it. His hot mess is no longer yours. If he wants to spin out, you are best waiting for the dust to settle before doing anything at all. This feels so much better — I know from experience.

Your ex may not have shitstorms and if he doesn't, great. Enjoy the calm. But if your ex does this, try dodging the shitstorm and waiting for it to pass. It will pass.

Exercise: Does your ex have shitstorms? How can you shield yourself?

Think about text/email/phone battles in which you got sucked into a shitstorm. How could you have set boundaries to keep yourself safe? What would it have been like if you did not engage with him at all? Think about how you can shield yourself moving forward and not engage when the storm starts building.

DON'T PUSH SEND.

You are going to write emails and texts which will feel absolutely brilliant to you and you are going to want to send them to your ex.

Don't send them.

Don't send them.

Don't send them.

And do not post them to Facebook or Instagram!

It's hard advice to take in, I know.

It's hard advice to follow. I know.

There will be times when he may bait you and you will want to reply immediately. Even then, do not reply immediately.

Before you reply to anything or send any email, ask yourself why you are sending it and what you hope to achieve by sending it. And then ask yourself and consult a friend and ask if the message you want to send achieves that purpose. If the answer is no, what you wrote has tremendous value and your ex does not deserve it. You cannot send it. That message was for you. You had something you needed to process, something you needed to say. You said it. The tree fell, and it may feel like nobody was there to hear it, but that's not true. The person who needed to hear it did in fact hear it. That person was you.

I have written dozens of these messages. And it took sending messages I should not have sent for me to learn this lesson. Let me save you the trouble —he doesn't have to hear it and in fact, it may make matters worse if he does. Sharing that innermost thought and feeling is not for him. He's not your husband anymore. He doesn't deserve that piece of you.

I learned this the hard way. My ex would bait me with emails. I would think that if I corrected his erroneous thinking, he would understand, and we would get along so much better. For the sake of the kids, I had to respond and remedy the situation. Or so I thought.

This is what actually happened. I would respond. My attempt to reason with him fueled his venom toward me. Tension built and he inevitably treated me with such disdain and contempt in front of the kids, even screaming and yelling at me, that my attempt to shield the kids ultimately had the opposite result.

Your communication with your ex now is vastly different from your communication when he was with your husband. Now, it serves your co-parenting relationship (if you have children) and divorce negotiations. That's it. You may want to mend fences and be friends and all that. And maybe that will happen for you and maybe not. But likely not now. Not now when you're in the midst of a divorce. It's not the time.

It is often said that you never divorce the same person you married — and there's a reason why it is often said.

Don't send any emails or text messages without considering whether or not it should be sent. That level of consideration takes at least a solid day.

Exercise: Create space for the messages you want to send but aren't going to.

Maybe it's a Notes App on your phone or a scratchpad in your purse. Decide where you're going to put the emails, notes, and messages that you feel compelled to write so they can sit in limbo until your judgment is better equipped to decide if it should be sent. Then start using it. Liberally.

IDENTITY CRISIS —
THE ONLY ASSHOLE HERE NOW IS ME.
WHO IS THAT?

With freedom comes time. And truthfully, there's so much to do that it may not feel like you have very much time. And you could probably fill all your time with the things that you usually leave undone so that you never have time to think about who you are and who you are becoming.

But don't. You need time to unwind and explore this new unmarried you. When you feel the weight of the time, it may feel heavy and overwhelming and even uncomfortable, which is so twisted because for so long, you probably craved time to yourself. Now you have it and it may not feel the way you had hoped. I've been there. I often waste time feeling guilty for not using my time more productively. It can be a challenge to not fill time. I'm getting better, and I am getting better at seeing the value of even 'wasted' time.

Much of what I once liked I don't like anymore. When I was married, I could watch hours of TV, and now I don't have the patience for that. Once upon a time, I needed TV to numb me so that I could pretend it wasn't as bad as it was. I don't want that anymore. Early in my divorce, I could barely focus long enough to read, which is symptomatic of the low-grade depression and PTSD I struggled with.

I wrote this book in short chapters because I imagine some of you reading it may struggle with the same thing. I have had to rediscover the things that feel healing and nurturing to me. You may find yourself having to do the same. The old stand-by may not work for you anymore. And that's okay. There are plenty of other things that will.

Everything you've thought about trying, try it.

I am not the same person as I was when I was married, and for a long time, I wasn't sure who I was becoming either. And that's okay. Over time, I discovered that I like grapefruit and tea and hot yoga and running in the rain. The list grew every day, and now that time has passed, I have a greater sense of who I am and who I want to be. It took a long time before I could enjoy a good television show again or focus on a book. And even when I watch TV or read, it's not the same as it was before. I am not who I was when I was married, and I am grateful for that. It took time and trying different things to get here.

Exercise: What do you know about yourself now that you didn't know then?

Who did you think you were when you were married and who are you now? How did you see yourself in the past, and who did you want to be at the time? How do you see yourself now, and who do you want to be? These are hard questions to answer, I know. It's okay to not have all the answers.

Start simply — what do you like to do and is it the same as what you thought you liked when you were married? Look at the small details — as small as grapefruit and tea. Those small details are bigger than you give them credit for. What do they mean to you? Dig deep. Appreciating a good grapefruit, going for runs, and turning off the television transformed me. What will transform you? What else do you want to try? When are you going to try it?

YOU GOT IT, GIRL.
BUT YOU'VE GOT IT ALL.
ON YOUR SHOULDERS.
HOLY HELL.

Big decisions are scary. Sometimes I want someone to consult with and tell me what they think I should do. But alas, I am on my own now. I can talk to friends but ultimately, I call the shots and nobody tells me what to do. I love that. And it terrifies me. I'm the only one driving this bus. If this bus crashes, it's all on me.

Finding my first rental house on my own was the first time I really felt the weight of having it all on me. I told myself that I might mess it up. I might make mistakes or make choices I'd come to regret. Nothing is irreversible. Nothing is permanent. My kids would be fine no matter which house I chose, and I would make peace with the choice I made. This is the anxious dance that was spinning through my head at the time. Making decisions like this on my own felt scary and empowering, both at once.

Even if you totally screw it up, you're going to be okay. It feels like life and death right now, but it's not. It's just a roof and walls — or whatever decision you're facing right now.

As for that first house, I had to find something during the holiday season. I picked a fantastic old restored craftsman in a quiet part of town that was a bit far but workable. Or so I thought. It was a nightmare — I ended up having kids in two different school systems and had to schlep all over town while trying to manage my business which was not near my home at all. It did not work. I did kind of screw it up.

But I have zero regrets because while living in that house, we got to know our neighbors Janet, Charles, and AJ next door. They brought my kids bubble wrap to stomp on and walked with us to the ice cream shop down the street. My kids don't have any grandfathers and Charles has stepped in and become one. It is an incredible gift. And while it may not have been the right house for us, it was the right house for that brief time in my life.

I am grateful for this misstep. We moved after living there for a year and a half. I think of that house now as our healing house. We still spend time with Janet, Charles, and AJ. Charles is the closest thing my kids have to a grandpa and that would not have been true if I hadn't made that mistake.

Exercise: What are you afraid of screwing up? What's the worst that can happen if you blow it?

Sometimes we feel paralyzed by the enormity of life decisions and we impart even larger significance to them than we need to. What decisions paralyze you? What would happen if you made a mistake? Would the world really end? Does it feel like it will?

THE DARK CLOUD.
YOU CANNOT STAY BENEATH IT.

There are times when I have felt this darkness looming. Everything feels dark. Everything feels hopeless. I can't see a way out from underneath the dark cloud, and it feels like it will be this way forever.

I see it in my clients. It's not divorce-specific, but divorce can definitely bring it on. The thing that really sucks about the dark cloud is that sometimes, you're feeling good and doing well and then there it is and it's like you're starting over, stuck beneath it all over again.

When the dark cloud is over you, fight against that urge to curl up and do nothing. Do something. Fight harder. Force yourself to do the things that you enjoy even if you're certain you won't enjoy them. Fight to get out from under the dark cloud. You will get out from under it.

And if you don't? Then you need reinforcements. You need to bring in the troops and this is so important. There's nothing wrong with you. You're good enough. You're strong enough. You're brave enough. But no army consists of only one soldier and that dark cloud is a fierce enemy. Getting help is not only about getting help for you — it's about getting help so that you can be who you need to be for your kids and family, for your friends, and most importantly, for you. They deserve that, and while you may not be able to see it right now, so do you.

If you've fought and you can't shake the dark cloud, find a therapist to help you. There are a lot of ways to do this. You can ask friends if they know any good ones. If that feels too vulnerable, go to *psychologytoday.com* and browse through the list of local therapists in your area.

Before you move forward with therapy, talk to the therapist and make sure you feel comfortable talking to them. If you don't, they aren't a good fit. The relationship is more healing than any homework your therapist assigns. Connection is key.

And if you think you can't afford therapy, there is always a way. Call the phone number on the back of your insurance card and request a list of in-network therapists. There are mental health clinics with sliding scales and excellent therapists almost everywhere if you do some research. Your employer's Employee Assistance Program (EAP) is another confidential and often totally free source for support.

Regardless of where I was with respect to the dark cloud, for several years, I had an annual appointment on the day before Thanksgiving with my therapist, because Thanksgiving was when the dark cloud haunted me the most. This past Thanksgiving was the first year that I didn't need to schedule that appointment.

If you're thinking you can't afford therapy right now, you can't afford not to go to therapy right now if that dark cloud is keeping you from functioning and enjoying your life. Quality therapy, and affordable therapy if you are struggling financially, is out there.

Exercise: What is the dark cloud like for you?

Have you struggled with any dark clouds and how have you managed? What helped and what didn't? If you are not under the dark cloud right now, keep the answer to what helped somewhere close. You may need it one day. Knowing what works for you when you feel that darkness is huge.

WORST CASE SCENARIO MIGHT BE BETTER THAN YOU THINK.

After months of trying to use a mediator to resolve my divorce and jumping through my ex's hoops, my ex informed me that he was taking me to court. My stomach sank and I felt like the world might end. I did not want to hire an attorney and fight him in court. I wanted it to be over.

It didn't take long before a friend of mine who had been through a divorce comforted me by telling me that I would probably be better off. That never occurred to me before that moment. I had so much fear wrapped around 'going to court' that I had never stopped to think about what that would actually mean for me. 'Going to court' would mean he could no longer threaten to take me to court, and it might actually push us closer to resolution which was all I wanted. Hiring an attorney would be expensive, but my bill to the mediator for not resolving things was not small.

This realization that the worst that can happen might not be so bad was a theme throughout my divorce. There was a time when the thought of losing my home was the worst possible thing I could imagine. Ultimately, letting go of that home was one of the very best things I did, and I was so glad when it was behind me. The fear I had wrapped up around having to let it go was enormous, far more painful than the pain of moving on, which was more liberating than anything else.

In hindsight, that moment when my ex threatened to take me to court was the catalyst that moved my divorce forward more quickly and, by the way, we did not end up in court.

Exercise: What is the worst case scenario? How bad is it _really?_

When you feel your stomach drop as the worst case scenario feels inevitable, take a moment to look at the reality of it. How much of your reaction is fear-based? What positive outcomes might you have neglected to consider? This is not an easy exercise, but it is a useful one. Think about the worst case scenarios you fear most and break them down. Is it as bad as you think?

SELLING THE HOUSE.
IT'S NOT A HOME.
IT'S WALLS AND A ROOF.

I remember early on in the divorce process, I read an article by a woman who said that she wished that she had let go of her house sooner. I remember thinking, "Not for me." I was wrong.

I remember the day I first saw the house we lived in. My daughter loved the backyard. We built a play structure for her back there and we painted it with the colors of the ocean. It looked like driftwood and when her siblings were born, they loved it too. Their artwork and photos were hung throughout the home. Their growth was charted on the door jam. I couldn't let that go.

But as financial pressures mounted and my ex became less willing to make financial sacrifices, I had to accept reality. I could not afford to stay there. It was a heartbreaking decision. But once I made it, it was freeing.

This was the house I built a life in. With my ex. He had a key. He had equity in it. It was not my home and it never could be. Selling it was exhausting and painful. Moving with kids sucks. But creating a home for myself and my kids that my ex was never a part of felt amazing.

Do I wish I had done it sooner? I don't think I could have. I did it when I was ready to do it. However, I share this story because having to sell a house or move is often part of the divorce process. It feels daunting.

I'm on the other side of it and it's not nearly as daunting and horrible as I feared. That article that woman wrote (I wish I knew what it was) gave me comfort and helped me to see a glimpse of hope where at the time I saw only pain. If you are in that place, I hope you can see a glimmer of hope too.

Once again, grief is part of the journey and grief is painful. If you are having to let go of a home that was meaningful for you, allow yourself to grieve the loss and know that when the grief passes, it will pave the way for a next chapter with a new home that you create without him.

Exercise: Create a home for your next chapter.

Take some time to reflect on the changes in your 'home'. Does it require letting go and grieving the home you built with your ex? Notice what that feels like and be gentle with yourself. What will the home of your next chapter be like? Envision it. What do you want your home to be like? Think less in terms of stuff and more in terms of values and energy.

DIVORCE HAS PERKS. ENJOY THEM.

I am heartbroken that I can't raise my children with their father as a married loving family. That's the part that cracks me open. It hurts. I wanted that and I don't get it. My friends who have it take it for granted. They see their monotonous sex lives and marital boredom and envy me because I get something that they don't.

If I want to play on an online dating website, I can. Guilt-free. If I want to flirt and play with cute men, I can. I get to have an exciting love life again — although, I must admit, it's not that exciting most of the time.

There are other perks. I get the whole bed to myself. Nobody is watching ESPN while I am trying to sleep. Dinner is whatever I want it to be. I call the shots. If I want a quiet night at home, I get a quiet night at home. The toilet seat is never left up (well, except when my son leaves it up). I don't have to trip over gigantic shoes anymore. The closet is mine and I don't have to make room for anyone else's stuff. My room is as I like it and as I keep it. I go to bed when I want and wake up when I want without worrying about disturbing anybody else or being disturbed by anyone else. If I snore, I don't have to worry about how it impacts anybody else and nobody will snore beside me. I can sleep naked if I want without it being perceived as an invitation for sex. I can watch anything I want on TV and I don't have to listen to MythBusters for the umpteenth time because my partner likes it.

There are perks. Lots of them. Find them. See them. Enjoy them.

Exercise: Write your perk list.

What are the perks of your divorce? What don't you miss? What do you enjoy about not being married anymore?

YOUR AMYGDALA IS TRAPPED IN YOUR CIVILIZED BODY. FIGHT, DON'T FREEZE!

The amygdala is your reptilian brain. It's the part of the brain that manages your survival instinct and fight, flight or freeze response. When we feel traumatized (and yes, divorce is trauma), the rational part of our brain goes off-line and the amygdala kicks into overdrive. But here you are, living a civilized life, sitting at your desk and watching TV on the sofa. Freezing is sometimes the easiest thing to do, but when you spend all of your time sedentary, stuck, and inert, you will feel sedentary, stuck and inert. That's not a good place to be.

A while ago, I told you to train for battle. Don't lose that fight. Hold on to it.

Every morning, wake up, get up, move forward. For me, the act of running feels like a survival response. There's a hill on my usual route and I feel like Rocky every time I run up it. I am fighting every time I push myself to run a little faster. I have also gone to kickboxing classes and the batting cages to release my anxiety. Engaging that fight response in a healthy way feels like you're pushing forward, you're winning. If hitting things doesn't appeal to you, it can be gentle. It can be as simple as walking forward or as Zen as yoga. Never underestimate the power of a soulful walk or a strong yoga pose.

Go kick ass. Divorce sucks, but you don't. Your amygdala wants to fight. Let it. You deserve to be a fighter. Freeze may feel easier but engage that fight response in whatever way feels right to you. Push yourself beyond that instinct to freeze and forge ahead instead.

Exercise: Assess your natural survival response.

What's your natural survival response? **Fight, flight or freeze?** How has it served you? How can you engage a healthy fight response? What activities feel like fight to you?

SECTION 2:

SEEKING SUPPORT

How to disconnect from your ex, navigate friendships, family, and holidays, and enjoy your own company

BUILD YOUR VILLAGE WISELY.

You will need to build a tribe to get through this. Having friends to confide in, have fun with and reach out to for help is critical. I have a handful of friends I call to bitch to when I feel overwhelmed, stressed or sad (thank you Callie, Maggie, Janine, Danielle, Mandy, Erica, Susan), and many more friends who I know are there if I need them and always offer a steady supply of support (thank you Rosetta, Jenny, Laurie, Cinnamon, Anna, Kathy, Betty, Heather, Emily, Patty…) But finding your village can be a challenge and the friends you expect to be there may not be the ones who show up for you right now.

Make sure you have friends who get it. Friends who seemed to get it before may not get it anymore. It's hard to understand the pain and suffering and joy and wonder that divorce brings when you haven't been through it. It may be hard to connect with friends who are stressed out about kitchen remodels or exotic vacations with their husbands. Try not to take it personally. For reasons that have nothing to do with you, they may not be the right friends to lean on right now. Don't punish them for being in a different place than you are. But that doesn't mean you can't have friends. Reach out and try to forge friendships with other people going through divorces if you can. They will likely get it more than most and having those confidants can be really meaningful.

Find friends in your village to go out and have fun with. Be careful not to isolate yourself. It's easy to want to hole up and hide and run away from the world. Believe me, I have been there and wanted that. But isolation is a huge risk factor for depression. Make sure you have friends you can go out and have fun with even if you don't talk about heavy topics. Enjoying activities, even with friends who don't always 'get it', is good for you.

Just a note of caution: beware of friends who require drugs or heavy alcohol use to have fun. Turning to substances to get through a divorce often creates more problems. Also, beware of 'friends' who want more than friendship from you. This is a vulnerable time — be careful around friends who might also want to sleep with you. When you have sex with a friend, you again may create more problems, which is the last thing you want or need going through this.

Ask friends for help when you need it. I needed lots of help to get through this. I had a garage cleaning party for my 41st birthday which was truly amazing — my friends showed up to help me clean out my garage. Surprisingly, it was an incredibly fun night and one I will never forget. The food was amazing — my friends each brought something yummy and I planked a salmon. We listened to music, laughed and threw out the junk from my former life.

The highlight of the night was building a fire in my chiminea and burning old love letters and sentimental knickknacks from my marriage. Watching it go up in flames with friends who support me felt fantastic. Later, we took a hammer to a wedding photo (put in a plastic bag first for safety) and smashed it to pieces. So much fun. There was a lot of laughter and I have never felt more supported and comforted than I did that night. Remember, people like to feel needed, so as much as you don't want to inconvenience them, they may actually enjoy being able to be there for you.

This journey has strengthened friendships that I didn't know could be so meaningful. And I have friends who I thought would be there who are not really there at all. Focus on the ones who are there. Every once in a while, I get caught up and wonder, "Why don't they call?" I feel a tinge of loneliness and I wonder why they aren't there.

I know what that sting feels like. It hurts a little bit, but the best thing you can do for you and for them is to give them a pass. They have their own stuff. It's easy to wonder why they aren't thinking about you, but life is overwhelming and they have their own challenges and obstacles too. Have compassion for friends who don't seem to be there. Everybody is fighting their own battles. Just because you don't see their battles doesn't mean they don't have them. You probably haven't been available for them either lately. Maybe you don't even know what their battles are right now, and that's fair because you have a lot going on.

Instead of dwelling on the ones who aren't there right now, appreciate the friends who are there for you. That kind of friendship is incredibly meaningful.

Lean gently. I say this because I know how heavy my divorce was, especially for those who have never gone down this path. Make sure you have plenty of friends to lean on so you don't burn anyone out. If they do seem burnt out, don't take that personally. This is why you need a village of friends to lean on. They can't all always be there. It's not possible. You are going through one of life's greatest stressors and quite likely more than one (with divorce often comes moving and other stressors). It's heavy. They can't always be with that heaviness. They shouldn't be. And one day, you won't be either.

If you don't have the friends you need for this journey, find them. The place to find them is not a bar. Look for support groups or meet-ups or activities that interest you. Challenge yourself to ask for phone numbers from people you might enjoy getting to know, or reach out to someone you like but haven't spent much time with. Making friends is hard at any age, but some of my now closest friends came as a result of my divorce. I met Janine running a 10k. She too was going through a terrible divorce and she is now one of my closest friends.

Exercise: Take a look at your village.

Who is in your village? Is it who you expected? Who would you like to add to your village? Do you need to reach out more for support? Do it.

PEOPLE SAY STUPID SHIT WHEN YOU ARE GETTING A DIVORCE. FORGIVE THEM.

I had a housekeeper for fifteen years. Let's call her Esmerelda. She was with me before I had kids and through both of my pregnancies. She's a kind, good-hearted woman and my children adore her. She was a shitty housekeeper. For years, my friends begged me to fire her. I am too loyal. She wasn't always a shitty housekeeper, but somewhere along the way, she stopped working as hard, and I am a terrible boss and a far shittier housekeeper than Esmerelda, so I never corrected her. I tell you this because as much as I loved Esmerelda, her words cut deep.

After years of hearing my friends beg me to fire Esmerelda because my house was not clean even while she was cleaning it, I finally had to fire her for financial reasons. It was just after my then-husband moved out. I told Esmerelda that we were having to let her go because we were splitting and could not afford her. "Children need both parents in the home with them," she explained to me. "I will pray for you. I will pray that your family doesn't split up. It will hurt your children too much." Screw you, Esmerelda. She voiced my greatest fear as though it was fact. I was terrified that this divorce would hurt my kids and then she said it would. It killed me to hear her say it.

Most people tend to be understanding. But sometimes people say annoying stuff like asking me, a therapist, if I had considered couples therapy. Umm, duh? Been there, done that. Our therapy bills could easily have bought a house in some states and might have put one of our kids through college.

There are certain things that people say, well-meaning, that suck. "Your poor kids." Yes, my poor kids. I am totally doing this to mess them up. "Marriage has its ups and downs." This implies that somehow I was not able to ride out the downs the same way they were when they have no idea what I went through. "I'm so sorry." Well, I'm not. Actually, your assumption that this divorce is such a horrible thing for me is bullshit. The truth is that this divorce is releasing me from a devil's bind that kept me imprisoned for years. Don't be sorry for me. Be excited for my next chapter. My children and I will find happiness in it.

Here's the thing about all of these things that people say. It's about <u>them</u>, not you. The way people react to divorce is based on what it brings up for them. Divorce means different things to different people. You don't know what goes on behind their closed doors just as they don't know what's going on behind yours. I feel certain that Esmerelda's husband has done horrible things that she endured for the sake of her children. If she let me off the hook for choosing to leave, it would somehow leave her on the hook for choosing to stay. The shit people say to you about your divorce has nothing to do with you most of the time. They are projecting their stuff on you. They can't help it. Try to have compassion for them. Divorce brings up so much for so many — memories from childhood or struggles in their present day relationships. They don't mean to be assholes. They can't help it.

And Esmerelda doesn't clean my house anymore.

Exercise: Rehearse what you want to tell people.

People are going to hear about your divorce. I was shocked to find out that a mother I had never met was asking about my divorce early on. So weird. They don't know what to say, but if you have something prepared with solid boundaries that feels comfortable to you, you're in good shape.

Early on, I had prepared this: "Well, I had always wanted to be a single mom and now that I'm about to turn 40, this seems like a good time to do it." At the time, this was all I could handle. A humorous dismissal. By the way, I never said it. But it felt good to know that I could.

A more effective and easily spoken response is something like this, "It's true. We're getting a divorce. It's the right decision for our family but it's obviously a hard time and we need space (or support?) while we get through it." This isn't what you tell close friends. It's what you say to friends with whom you need to keep some boundaries.

Work on responses that feel right to you. Remember them. They will come in handy.

SPLITTING THE FRIENDS

That fear that you may lose friends is totally legit and one of the bitter realities of divorce. You may. And you have some control, but not a lot because most of your friends have a stronger connection to one of you over the other already. That will play a huge role in how the friends split plays out.

The day I told my ex to leave, I texted two of our mutual friends and told them that he was going to need them. Years before we had kids, we all played softball together and after we had kids, my ex was able to continue playing and I was not (the games were not close to where we lived). They were mutual friends who we didn't see often, friends we had prior to having kids, and friends I adored. I knew he needed them more than I did, and I also knew that my local friends valued my friendship and would be there for me no matter what happened.

I didn't really feel the loss of any friendships until I was invited to a birthday party in the circle of friends that I reached out to when I told my ex to leave. I went to that party after not having seen any of those friends since before the split. I knew my ex was attending as well but felt confident we could avoid each other and manage to celebrate our friend's milestone birthday in perfect harmony. It was not my finest thinking.

The party was incredibly awkward for me. I realized I had not seen any of these friends recently and was disconnected from them, and I had no idea what they thought or made up about me and the end of my marriage. And that was uncomfortable. Truthfully, I don't think most of them were thinking about me at all — they were enjoying the party as people do.

But my anxiety over this disconnect brought me to the bar and I had too many drinks and when someone I hadn't seen in a while cornered me in the bathroom, also having had a few too many drinks, asking me about my marriage, I overshared. I felt confident she would hold my secrets but stupidly didn't think about the fact that there were other people in the bathroom too. I left the bathroom wondering who heard me overshare and then I felt more uncomfortable. I had to stay long enough to sober up and I felt awkward every minute of it.

Meanwhile, my ex socialized with friends he had seen several times since our split. Being around him furthered my discomfort. I was awkward when I talked to old friends who, I am certain, felt my discomfort.

And then I drove away wishing I had never gone to the party, because while these people will always be people I care about and people who cared about me, they were going to be his friends. I decided that the day I texted and asked them to be there for him and not for me.

A friend of mine tried to maintain a friendship with a mutual friend of her ex. It didn't go well. Conversations this mutual friend had with her ex sometimes felt like betrayals and she felt judged by this mutual friend who was hearing her ex's point-of-view. Even in amicable divorces, friendship shares are tough to negotiate and don't often go smoothly.

Friend splits are like amputations — lost limbs with phantom pains. I don't think it's possible to make it through a divorce without at least some amputations but try to keep the friendships that are most important to you. I miss those old friends sometimes. I do. And maybe I will be able to reconnect with some of them someday or play softball with them. Or maybe not. Either way, I am very grateful for the friendships that I still have in my life.

Exercise: Reflect on friendships.

Think about the friendships you value most. Reach out to the friends you value most and let them know that their friendship is meaningful to you. It's important to reach out to the friends you don't want to lose now so that they know you want them in your life.

OTHER AMPUTATIONS — THE EX'S FAMILY.

Figuring out how to forge relationships with the ex's family can be challenging. If you don't have children, there are no long term ties that continue to bind you to that family. However, if you do have kids, your ex's family will forever be a part of your children's lives. Either way, moving forward and continuing or letting go of those relationships may be hard.

Maybe you loved them. They cared for you and made you family. But now they aren't. Their relationship and need to support their child make your relationship more challenging. It's a loss and you may have to grieve it. It's normal to feel the pull and pain of the grief.

Maybe you didn't love them. It's a relief that you don't have to deal with them anymore. Their drama is not your circus. No more trips for uncomfortable visits, no more painful conversations, no more tension in a home that didn't feel like home.

Or maybe you loved them and you didn't love them. I know that sounds like a contradiction, but feelings are wild that way — they often contradict each other. And that's okay too. You may have loved them sometimes and valued their relationships at times, and also feel some relief of letting go of their circus. But the push/pull of those feelings can be confusing. When my mother-in-law's health was declining, I sometimes thought I should go visit her, and then I thought about how much I shouldn't go visit her, almost simultaneously. When she died, I wanted to go to her funeral and I didn't want to go, all at the same time. I did go, and while it was nice to connect and give hugs to people I considered family at one time, I left early because it was uncomfortable too.

Negotiating relationships with the ex's family is confusing. Keep healthy boundaries. It is hard to accept that some of his family may cut you off for reasons that are out of your control but finding that acceptance helps.

Exercise: Journal on your relationships with your ex's family.

What was your relationship like with his family? What is it likely to be like in the future? Is there any grief or sadness around that? It's understandable if there is. Allow yourself to feel it.

MIRROR NEURONS ARE SCARY. BE CAREFUL.

Have you ever noticed how sometimes people who have been married a while start to look like they are related? There's a scientific explanation for it and you need to know it because you don't want your kids to have a bitter and angry resting face.

Our need to connect to people is so deeply hardwired that there is actually a physical component. Our faces mirror the faces of the people we spend time with. It's instinctual. Over time, the muscular changes in our faces as a result of this mirroring causes us to develop wrinkles and facial expressions that resemble the people we care about. The most striking example I have noticed of this phenomenon is my half-sister who was put up for adoption immediately after birth. I didn't know her until she was an adult. I saw a photograph of her with her adoptive mother and saw something quite remarkable — they have the same smile despite the fact that they share no genetics whatsoever. Mirror neurons did that.

Why is this important? I have been thinking a lot about mirror neurons lately. I think about how my children mirror what I show them and how I am actually making an imprint on the lines and expressions on their face every day. It's pretty powerful stuff. I also think about all of the time I spent searching to connect with my ex and how I don't want to look like him. I am done mirroring him and his expressions. I am letting go of that. My face will not be his.

Think about mirror neurons and see what comes up for you. It's pretty powerful stuff. You choose who you spend time with in life so, in a way, you choose the lines on your face. I am so grateful to surround myself with such amazing friends who I genuinely admire and would be honored to mirror. But part of getting a divorce is releasing myself from any obligation to mirror people who aren't healthy for me.

Notice that I say 'people' and not just him. Divorce is an opportunity to clean house. Let go of the friendships or relationships that don't serve you in a healthy way now. You need to surround yourself with healthy people, because those are the people you want to look like and you want your children to look like. Think of the imprint the people you surround yourself with are making on the lines of your face and on the faces you care about.

> ### *Exercise: Mirror, mirror on the wall. Who do you look like?*
>
> Who do you want to look like? Think about the friends you surround yourself with and what they will do to the structure of your face. Do they smile? Does their face reflect a lifetime of laughter? Who do you want your children's faces to look like? How can you find more time to spend with those people?

LOOK FOR THE HELPERS.

When going through my divorce, I saw ugliness. Divorce often brings out the worst in people. In the midst of our divorce, I discovered a side of my ex that I hadn't fully seen before. There were times when it felt like it wasn't only about my ex— it was all humanity. Men. I heard stories of friends going through divorces and felt like every story was confirmation of the brutal reality I was coming to accept. If you feel as I did, look again.

When there's a disaster or senseless tragedy, there's a quote by Fred Rodgers which circulates the internet regularly: "When I was a boy and I would see scary things in the news, my mother would say to me, 'Look for the helpers. You will always find people who are helping.'" I love this quote every time I see it. I am continually touched by people's kindness when I look for it. Don't get me wrong, I have found that friends who I thought would be supportive have been absent, but I have also found that it's my own fault more than theirs. I don't reach out and tell them I am lonely and struggling. They are busy with their own lives and perhaps fighting battles I don't know about too.

But when I have reached out, I have been blown away by the kindness and support of my friends. A friend from my softball team kindly helped me get my divorce filing in order. Upon hearing that I was selling my house and had no idea where my kids and I would live the following month, another friend on my softball team offered to let my kids and me stay with him and his family. I reached out to a single mom friend I don't know well, and she eagerly met me for coffee and gave me input on my divorce. I mentioned to a friend that I have been lonely, and she sent me texts checking on me. My therapist gives me hugs which is a huge comfort. When I had to move, friends came on my birthday and spent the night helping me clean out my garage. When I see friends' husbands, they are kind and warm and supportive, which feels reassuring that not all men are like the one I left.

There may be days when you will only be able to see the assholes in the world. Divorce can make for a gloomy lens. But try to see the helpers. And when you need it, ask for help. You may feel like you are burdening them, but the opposite is true — people like to feel needed. You may be surprised by how many people would like to support you and don't know how to do it.

You need help right now, and not only because you are going through hell. You need help to remind you that there are helpers and kind people in your life. You have chosen good people to be your friends even if the husband you chose did not work out. And if you don't have those friends in your life, it's time to make them because you're worth it.

Exercise: Be grateful for the helpers.

Take a moment and write down the names and gestures that have been helpful and kind to you.

HOLIDAYS ARE LIKE UNPOPPABLE PIMPLES.

** I first wrote this chapter during my first Thanksgiving amidst divorce. To give you some context, I stupidly offered to cook Thanksgiving dinner and invited my ex to join. My mother and her date did not come until dinner time. The ex went for a long leisurely bike ride and showed up to eat. My twins were only two and a handful. I was busting my ass cooking a full Thanksgiving dinner by myself while watching my three kids only to have my ex and family show up at dinner time ready to be fed. I wrote this chapter during that time and I didn't change it because while it's not pretty, it's how I felt that day and it is real…

I do not feel grateful this year.

You will be grateful. I will be grateful. Sometimes. But not every day. Not every holiday. And definitely not today. Today sucks. Because holidays sometimes suck. Holidays can be a reminder of how grateful you 'should' feel. I didn't tell many friends (except for one going through a divorce who was also miserable) how much my Thanksgiving really sucked. They wouldn't understand. They would tell me how grateful I should be. And I am. Sometimes. But not today. And being told that I should feel grateful when I feel guilty that I am not more grateful makes me want to punch someone.

Holidays are hard.

Be kind to yourself even if you don't feel grateful or however else other people want you to feel or worse yet, tell you that you should feel.

Holidays are sometimes a harsh and loud reminder of how different things are from how you want them to be. I want the Thanksgiving filled with family and fun, not the one where I slave away at the stove cooking a turkey dinner not one of my children wants to eat trying to keep my kids from killing each other without any adult company at all. A friend of mine struggled with a different loss over the holidays — she felt the loss of her husband's family who she often spent holidays with. This didn't come up for me because I didn't spend holidays with my in-laws. But it can be sad when your relationships with extended family change as a result of your divorce. All of it can really suck. I spent Thanksgiving texting with someone else going through a divorce about how bitter and ungrateful I was. The upside was that I felt gratitude that she was able to be there and have that conversation with me. I guess there was something to be thankful for after all.

Holidays bring grief to a head like a painful cystic pimple, but it doesn't pop. It festers. There's nothing you can do to make the holiday stop except wait for it to pass and heal on its own. And wait for the next pimple because those holidays keep coming, year after year.

Just remember, no matter how painful it is, it won't always be this bad. And you will always be bigger and stronger than a pimple for whatever that's worth.

** I should note that the Thanksgiving the following year was fantastic. I write about that and how I pulled that off in the next chapter. Despite my bitterness when I wrote this, it does get better. I chose to keep this chapter though because it's okay to not always be grateful and happy and sunshine and rainbows.

Exercise: Have you suffered through any holidays post-divorce?

If you have struggled through any holidays, take a moment to be compassionate with yourself. It was hard. It will get easier.

You might also want to start thinking about what you want holidays to look like moving forward in terms of custody. This part isn't easy, so be gentle with yourself and reach out to your village for support.

THE SECRET TO SURVIVING HOLIDAYS.

One of the pieces of divorce that sucks is having to let your kids spend holidays with your ex and not getting to have them with you where they belong. Waking up on a holiday without kids is not easy and nothing I tell you will make that part easier, but there are tricks to making it survivable.

If you lose a holiday, keep the ritual and move the day or time. Or create a new ritual to replace it, one that's more flexible, and schedule it so that it's special around your time with your kids. I am writing this on Easter Sunday. In years past, I planned elaborate brunches with friends, shared mimosas and planned egg hunts. Today, my kids are not with me. I get them back later today to take them to a Dodgers game and I am excited for that. At first, I was going to abandon the egg hunt altogether, but it's a ritual I enjoy and my daughter begged me to continue it. I usually make it a game, hiding pieces of a map to treasure in eggs or something fun like that. We don't have much time for it, but I planned an Easter egg hunt with a decoder so that they can find their treasure before we head off to the game.

The morning without them is uncomfortable as the Easter bunny is at the bakery down the street from me and I cannot take my kids to see him, but it is not excruciating and in fact, I am enjoying a cup of coffee and some quiet. I have not yet had to give up a Christmas morning but if or when I do, Santa will simply come to our house a day early or a day late. I will not give up the ritual of Christmas morning no matter what because participating in that ritual with my kids is meaningful to me. I don't have to give it up because that day of the year is not one when I get to have my kids. I can move the ritual if I want to.

My first Thanksgiving during the process of divorce was horrible. (I wrote about it, so you know). The following year, I did it differently. I allowed my ex to take the kids for Thanksgiving dinner and I enjoyed Thanksgiving brunch with them. I let them choose anything they wanted to eat, so we had monkey bread, sausage, and bacon with fruit. It was fantastic. And then they went to their dad's house and I went for a long hike by myself. I ate no turkey. I did not try to make my kids eat turkey. I had the best Thanksgiving in many years, and I am so grateful that I created a new ritual that worked for me and worked for my kids, and that felt like fun and joy rather than loss and struggle.

Rituals are meaningful. Letting go of them can be excruciating, so don't do it. You may need to tweak, change or reschedule them, but you don't have to give up holiday rituals. If anything, I suggest creating more ritual in your life, not less. Consider changing rituals when necessary to suit you and to make them more enjoyable for you and your family.

Exercise: Preserve and create holiday rituals for you and your family.

Think about the rituals that are important to you and consider how you can be flexible and keep them even with custody shifts. Does it mean changing the date and celebrating Christmas a week early or does it mean changing the ritual to one that you enjoy and letting go of one that never worked for you? Rethink your holidays and make them something to look forward to rather than something to dread.

TO TRASH OR NOT TO TRASH.
SPEAKING OF THE EX...

In my experience, I feel more confident when I hold my boundaries and I am mindful of what I tell people about my divorce. Notice I haven't written anything splashy about my ex-husband in this book. That is not accidental.

Yes, there is a part of me that wants to tell every sordid detail of our marriage to see the reaction on someone's face and feel their sympathy. I don't do it. It's not because I need to protect him. It's because I don't want people talking about it and I don't want my children to suffer from gossip about their dad. And I don't want to make their father's life more difficult because doing so would make my children's lives more difficult too.

While I of course have those close friends who know everything and keep it in their vault, I don't tell people very much. These are the rules I have come up with on the subject that help guide me in determining what to share with who:

It's not my job to protect him anymore from the consequences of his choices. Am I trying to protect him?

Do I want people talking about this? If the answer is no, I don't share it with anyone except extremely close friends.

Would it impact my children adversely if people knew? How would they feel if they heard about this from a friend?

One of the greatest compliments I received in my divorce was from a mom I respect but don't know well. She texted me and said she heard about the divorce and was impressed that we were still loving and respectful. I don't feel loving toward my ex, but I am thrilled that I am not making a scene for my kids to have to suffer through.

Exercise: What do you want to tell and to whom? Set your boundaries.

Take a moment to reflect on what you want to tell people and what is off limits. How do you hold those boundaries? How does it feel to hold them?

DATE YOURSELF.

Spend time getting to know you again. Plan an evening for yourself as though you were your date. Maybe it means a bubble bath with candles and a good book. Or a walk. Or a hike. Or a meal out. Or a movie. A massage? Anything. It can be anything. But plan it and look forward to it and if you have a glass of wine, let it be a good one and enjoy it. Don't get drunk though — this assignment isn't about having a drunken pity party. It's about enjoying time alone. Once you start to enjoy your own company, you may discover, as I have, that you really like it.

This assignment is important. When you feel like you need somebody else there to be able to enjoy yourself, it puts you in a precarious spot. If you need someone to be able to enjoy yourself, you will be desperate to find someone so that you can enjoy yourself, and that sets you up to pine over some loser who isn't right for you. You can do better — get to know yourself first.

Yes, spend time with friends. That's good too. But date yourself. Learn to enjoy your own company and look forward to time by yourself too. It's more important than you realize, and it may be different than you expect. Not having to negotiate or worry about what other people want to do is incredibly nice. I just enjoyed a wonderful weekend by myself. I needed to recharge. Got a poke bowl on Friday and watched a movie. Got a massage on Saturday and folded laundry while watching a show and enjoying a glass of red wine. I am relaxed and refreshed.

Exercise: Plan a date. Fill it with some of your favorite things.

You can do anything you want. You don't need to please anybody but you. If this feels uncomfortable, notice the discomfort and let it be. Allow yourself to enjoy a night with yourself even if it feels uncomfortable or strange to you.

SECTION 3:

BE A BAD-ASS SINGLE PARENT

Minimizing the Likelihood of Screwing Up Your Kids:
Kids, Custody, Co-parenting

THE QUIET HOUSE.

There are few things more painful than when the ex takes the kids and you come home to a quiet house. We gradually stepped up my ex taking the kids and every additional night felt like torture. I became this needy, sad shell of myself. I wanted to curl up in a ball and shrink away. My way of coping was to overdose on yoga, swipe through a dating website and distract myself utterly and completely so that I didn't have to think about how lonely and quiet it was without my children there.

It hurt. It really did. The kind of ache that you feel in your body. They should be home. They should be with me. And they were not there. And I could not protect them. Or love them. And it was so hard.

If you have difficulty with the quiet, consider it time for reflection. Notice the sting and let it go. Let it open the door to growth.

There is a flip side to the quiet house. After a while, it becomes a taste of freedom. You can do and be who you want to during that time without worrying about babysitters or chasing children. It's an opportunity to pick up lost hobbies, connect with friends, and take care of yourself. When I started to feel the freedom of it, I also felt a wave of guilt for enjoying it. I felt guilty looking forward to a quiet morning of not having to get my kids ready for school and instead getting to go for a jog without a care in the world. I felt guilty for not being there for my kids and not being sure if they needed me there or not. And yet, there's nothing I can do about that.

So listen, straight up, that empty house, it does hurt. Especially in the beginning. And it gets better. But it always hurts a little in some twisted way. For me. And maybe not for you. And that's okay. Enjoying the freedom, if and when you get to that place, is a very good thing. You have nothing to feel guilty for (I have to remind myself of that too). After everything you've been through, you deserve that. Enjoy it.

Exercise: What are your lost hobbies? What books do you want to read? What will fuel your growth in the quiet moments?

Take some time to explore what you've let go of and can reclaim for yourself. Then reclaim it.

KIDS ARE RESILIENT BUT YOU CAN TOTALLY MESS THEM UP. WATCH OUT.

The first time I considered ending my marriage, I was so terrified of screwing up my kid (at the time, I only had one) that I called child development experts looking for advice. I was not a therapist at the time. I am an anxious person, an imperfect perfectionist which is anxiety-provoking in and of itself. I wanted to do it right. I got advice and some of it helped, but what I have learned over the years of being both a therapist and a mom is that no matter what I do, I will make choices that will impact my children and maybe even mess them up. Maybe a lot. Maybe a little. Even if I do my best.

No parent ever thinks, "Gosh, I'd really love to screw up my kids with this divorce," and yet I often see that impact of divorce on my clients in my therapy practice. There are some things you can do to minimize the damage.

First, don't put your feelings on them. When I made the decision to divorce, I was prepared to give a full serious talk. But then a therapist explained this to me: children only really want to know how it directly impacts them. In their eyes, the world revolves around them. They don't care about the nature of your marital relationship or your feelings about the break-up. However, if you are sobbing and convey to them that this is extremely upsetting, they will feel the upset as strongly as you do and may be very scared. That does not help them.

It's worth repeating: Do not put your feelings on them.

When we told my older daughter, we explained to her that dad was going to live somewhere else. We explained that he would still come over almost every morning and every weekend which was pretty much as it had been since he worked so much anyway. At first, my daughter was furious and yelled, but then we explained that it wasn't much different than how it had been and that instead of sleeping on the sofa, dad would be on a bed in an apartment five minutes away.

She calmed down quickly. Don't get me wrong -- she told everyone she knew at school about our split and struggled with the news. It hit her. But she wasn't broken. Now, years later, when I ask her if our divorce was difficult for her, she says 'no'. She's twelve now and maybe she will tell her therapist something different, but while I have seen my daughter struggle through other issues, she doesn't cry about having divorced parents. My twins were only two at the time. They didn't understand. And they have never really known different. And that's okay.

Kids think the world is about them, so everything good is about them but everything bad is also about them. If you don't spell out that this is not their fault and it is not the result of anything they have done, they are likely to assume responsibility for stuff they never had any control over. I have a friend who as a young girl borrowed her father's jacket because she was cold and for years thought the heart attack that killed him a few hours later that night was her fault because she made him cold. If you can keep your child from feeling responsible for your failed marriage, do it. Tell them explicitly that it is not their fault even if you think they know that already. It's too much for any little person to have to carry around.

Do not give them too much information. They don't need details. Kids who are enmeshed (in other words, kids who are made to be mom or dad's best friend through this) grow up feeling that they need to caretake for others and often become resentful of the parent who enmeshed them. They do not need the details of your divorce. My daughter pressed me. She wanted to know why. I didn't tell her. I told her it was a grown-up matter and she didn't need to worry about it. Don't you wish you didn't have to wrap your mind around your own broken marriage? Your children deserve at least that. Don't ever put your spouse's baggage on their plate no matter how old or mature they seem. Eventually, she pressed, and I gave her a hazy answer that was 100% truth but vague enough that she didn't have to hold the excruciating details of the whole truth.

The other stuff you know. Don't trash their other parent even when you want to. Be careful what you say to friends in their presence. Try not to yell at your ex in front of them. Don't put them in the middle of your divorce. You know this stuff.

And you can't control your spouse. He might say or do horrible things. Don't one-up him. Be the level parent who stays the course and offers a secure base. Then when the kids are in bed, call a friend and bitch all you want. Or write another fuck you letter if you need to. I am not telling you not to feel bitter and angry. But you need to make sure that you are not putting your bitterness and anger on your kid.

One last time: do not put your feelings on your kids. Let them be a kid.

I genuinely believe that divorced homes can be the best thing for children when the marriage was unhealthy or unkind. While I have clients who suffered as a result of their parents' divorce, I have many clients who have difficulty with healthy relationships because they grew up watching their parents' unhealthy one. Divorce can be character-building and an opportunity to teach your children about growth, boundaries, and healthy relationship skills.

Exercise: Take responsibility for how your divorce has bled to your kids and clean it up — it's not too late.

Think about the boundaries you set around your divorce for your kids. How is your divorce impacting them? How can you do better? What have you done well? Take a moment to view your divorce through their eyes, letting go of all of the emotional baggage. What's it like? How are your kids doing? If you're not sure, ask them, but if you ask them, do it in a sincere way without communicating that you're asking because they should be upset. Are they upset about your divorce? Or are they upset because they see you upset? Or are they maybe not upset at all?

CUSTODY. PREPARE TO BE GUTTED.

Letting go of the care of your children is excruciatingly painful no matter how you do it. It's the reason many people stay in bad marriages — they don't want to deal with having to share custody of their children with their ex.

If you have stayed home with the kids and perhaps envision an arrangement in which you have more than 50/50 custody, unless your ex agrees to this, you will have a fight on your hands. From everything I have been told, the courts in most areas favor 50/50 arrangements.

Often, parents will argue that they are the better parent and that their children are happier in the home with them. Guess what? The law doesn't care. A family law attorney once told me something that really stuck, that even serial killers get visitation. Unless your children have literally been abused by their parent, it is hard to get more than 50/50 if the other parent wants 50/50.

A friend of mine divorced an addict when their daughter was very young. He passed drug tests mandated by the court when he knew he had to take them and strung together some resemblance of sobriety for periods of time. She did not feel her daughter was safe in his care. She spent tens of thousands of dollars fighting for more than 50/50 custody and the fight took years. She tells me she doesn't regret that money spent because it gave her years to keep her daughter safe until her daughter was at an age when 50/50 didn't feel as frightening to her. Eventually, he did get 50/50. I think her child was four or five at the time and my friend felt much better about it.

Recently, a friend called me, upset because her kids have such a hard time with her ex's poor parenting and don't like spending time at his house. He can be mean and ignores them when they are at his house. But nobody cares. Right now, the court wants 50/50 unless the children are in danger. (Consult your attorney to confirm this is true where you live. I am not an attorney and can offer no legal advice). Arguing over who is the better parent is fruitless, because the courts don't care unless someone is abusive.

But that doesn't mean you don't fight. I did not spend tens of thousands of dollars fighting like my friend did, but I did not sign over 50/50 custody when my twins were two either. I knew it wasn't what was best at the time. We gradually moved toward that and my little ones were almost five by the time my ex had 50/50 custody. I am glad the transition was slow because I genuinely believe that's what my kids needed.

On the flip side, you may want 50/50 and your ex may not be a safe parent. For instance, if your ex is spinning out of control post-divorce and using substances, you may need to advocate for your kids' safety. Is he driving them drunk or getting blasted while 'watching' the kids? During the course of your marriage, you may have convinced yourself that these behaviors weren't that bad, but you were bullshitting yourself. Don't bullshit your kids.

If your kids aren't safe, it's your job as a parent to protect them even if your ex hates you for speaking up. It's common for parents wanting an 'amicable divorce' to avoid difficult conversations for fear of ruffling feathers. Sometimes, that's okay. You don't need to go to war over everything. But if it impacts your children's safety or well-being, that's another story. They need to feel safe more than they need your divorce to be friendly. If you are acting as though an unsafe parent's behavior is acceptable, you are confusing your children.

> ### *Exercise: Brainstorm about custody.*
>
> If you are in the midst of a fight over custody, spend some time reflecting on how you want this to look and how it will likely look. Does it match up? If it does not match up, reflect on the disparity. Are your kids safe? Do you need to advocate for them? Or do you want to drag your heels? Consult with an attorney as this is not legal advice since I am not a lawyer.

CO-PARENTING WITH SOMEONE WHO YOU SOMETIMES SECRETLY WISH WAS DEAD IS NOT EASY.

Nobody tells you how hard this is. They tell you how important it is, but they don't tell you how much of a challenge it can be. Even the word 'co-parenting' can feel like an impossibility depending on your ex. There is no 'co' anything when someone is unwilling to consider anything besides their own best thinking.

One night, I was driving my kids home just before dinner time and I stopped for gas at a station with a convenience store. My daughter said to me, "Why don't we just get dinner here?" And then it occurred to me — my kids eat dinner at gas stations with their dad sometimes.

Many parents watch their child get a little chubbier and start drinking soda following a divorce. You can't control what happens at the other parent's house.

If your ex is open to genuine co-parenting and is capable of hearing you without getting wounded and attacking, hooray. Take advantage of it.

If your ex lashes out at you and co-parenting is not so simple, I get that too. You may have to tread gently, and I highly recommend that you focus on keeping your side of the street in order. If something is happening at his house that genuinely concerns you, send a very concise and unemotional email alerting your ex to your concern. Avoid any attacking language and keep your concern to the facts of what you know.

For example, instead of, "You are acting like an asshole when you yell at the fucking umpire at our kid's games and you're making it harder on her," try, "I am worried about how your behavior impacts our child when you become angry with the umpire."

Notice the 'I' statement. When you talk to someone with 'you' statements, they will be defensive and reactive. They can't really help it — it's how most people are wired, you and I included. Shifting to an 'I' statement and focusing on your feeling in a way that doesn't assign judgment or blame lessens the likelihood of a nasty reaction. He might still react poorly and lash out, but you'll know you handled it cleanly and that's important. You can let go.

And that's the hardest part. Letting go. You cannot control what happens on his time with the kids. All you can do is show up, be present and offer as much as you can to your kids on your time. You cannot control whether or not your ex yells at your daughter's coaches or umpires (or whatever bad behavior he engages in that impacts your kids). As unpleasant and often painful as that sometimes is to watch, all you can do is let go and tolerate the discomfort of letting go.

If they come to you with concerns about what happens at their father's home, validate their feelings when appropriate and address them as best you can. Don't deny their reality, but don't trash talk their dad either. It's a fine line but an important one. If it's something that worries you, bring it up to your ex using 'I' statements as much as possible. That's about all you can do.

Exercise: How could you co-parent more effectively?

Do you use 'you' statements when speaking with your ex? Do you trigger a defensive reaction in him? How do you attempt to co-parent? What works and what doesn't? What do you need to let go of?

DON'T SHORTCHANGE YOURSELF. YOU CAN DO IT YOURSELF.
ALL OF IT.

A mother and friend I admire greatly decided she wanted to build a shoe rack for her heels in her closet using crown molding. She learned to use a power saw and she did it. How awesome is that?

While I am not using power tools with quite that level of sophistication, I have chosen to take some risks myself. One summer, I loaded my kids up (two three-year-olds and a nine-year-old) and flew to Portland for a long weekend. It was not without hiccups — we missed our flight out. There was no curbside baggage check and it was simply not possible for me to wheel a stroller, two pieces of checked baggage and all of our carry-ons by myself while managing my three children. I did not allow enough time and I learned that the hard way.

And yes, I bawled my brains out in the airport when they refused to put me on the next flight because there were no more mileage award tickets on that flight. And while there was a rude ticket lady who fed me the company line, someone kind decided to be kind and got me on that next flight anyway. We got there, we did it, we had a great time.

My children will always have that trip. I will always have that trip. It was hard but totally worth it. We hiked to the top of Multnomah Falls in Oregon. It was not easy. One of my littles made me carry her for most of the hike and there were a lot of switchbacks. But it was worth it to get to the top, look down and know that we did it. We made it there. My sister and I hiked with five kids (my niece and nephew in addition to my own) and we made it. Together. It was invigorating.

Some things are more challenging as a single parent, but that doesn't mean you shouldn't do them anyway. Enlist help if you need it. A client once told me about her parents' divorce and how the worst part of it was that they stopped doing things as a family. I don't want my children to ever feel that. And I don't want that either. Portland was hard. The flight back, all my kids were a wreck, especially my oldest. My son had a fever the night before and hadn't slept so was constantly on the verge of a meltdown. But we made it. I got a high-five from a dad who got it and another guy on the plane gave me a 'good job, mom' and I felt like a rock star. It wasn't a perfect trip. There were tantrums and a sleepless night. But I did ask for help. And I got it. And we did it. And I have no regrets.

I have taken road trips with my posse. I have spent hours in the car with them while they fought, whined and complained. I will keep trucking, no matter how challenging it may be. And it won't always be perfect.

But nobody can take it away.

Go do it. You <u>can</u> do it. Anything. If it's important to you. It might not always be easy but easy is not what matters.

Exercise: What do you want to do that feels impossible as a single mom? What would it look like to make it possible and do it anyway?

What adventures would be meaningful for you? What hobbies? Do you want to learn to use power tools? What around the house might you have delegated to a husband that you could manage and take care of yourself? What trips or experiences do you want to share with your kids and what would tackling that alone be like? If it's too much for one person to swing alone, is there a friend or family member who can help you make it happen?

DON'T PRETEND YOU
DON'T HAVE FEELINGS
TO PROTECT YOUR KIDS.

When you pretend you don't have feelings but your kids can tell that something is wrong, they will imagine that it's about them. Kids are egocentric, meaning they think the world is about them. It's not a defect in character — it's just the way kids think. If you tell them you're fine and you're not, they may make up that you are unhappy and displeased with them. That doesn't protect them from anything.

This doesn't mean you put your feelings on them and make them your buddy — you do not want to enmesh your kids. But you also don't want to send the message that it's not okay to have feelings or that you have to pretend and hide feelings from people you care about. Make sure they know that you have a support system and grown-up friends who are helping you deal with your difficult feelings. Sharing with them that you will be okay even if you are struggling with some difficult emotions, modeling moving through pain successfully, is a huge lesson for your kids.

You may think they don't know you are hurting. You are wrong. They may not understand it, but kids feel that there is something amiss. They know. They worry. You can't help it.

The answer is not to process your feelings with your kids and tell them all about why you are hurting. Please don't do that. That kind of enmeshment confuses people. I hear about it from adults on my couch all the time who are still trying to sort through the enmeshment they endured as kids. Your kids are not there to help you solve your problems.

The best you can do is allow yourself to feel and let them know you are feeling sad or hurt or frustrated and it has nothing to do with them. If you notice that you are more irritable with them or with others as a result of your feelings, let them know this so they understand. "I'm feeling sad. It's not about anything you've done. Mommies have feelings too and I will be okay, but I'm a little more grumpy than usual so go easy on me." Adjust it for the age of your child or children and don't do this every day. You don't get a free pass for being an asshole every single day. And when you do take it out on them, apologize as you would if they were a full-sized human you had treated poorly. It teaches them that they don't need to be perfect, but they do need to repair. Don't beat yourself up for losing your shit — it's an opportunity to teach them a life lesson if you take responsibility and do it right.

This is a dance. Allowing your kids to see you are human and experience difficult feelings as they do while still maintaining boundaries and assuring your children they are safe can be a challenge. You may not always do it perfectly but teaching your children it's okay to be imperfect and letting them know when you have been imperfect is huge. If you blew it and you were a jerk to your kids but you own it and take responsibility, you're doing great. It's hard. So hard. I know. I struggle with this too.

Exercise: Establish healthy boundaries with your kids.

How are you managing your feelings in the presence of your kids? Are you hiding them, or sharing too much? Take some time to reflect on the boundaries you want to set with them and consider how you let them know you have feelings and are dealing with them but will be okay.

MAKE PEACE WITH THE MESS. DON'T BEAT UP YOURSELF OR YOUR KIDS FOR IT.

When you are a single mom, it all falls on you. Taking out the trash, the cooking, the cleaning, the laundry, replacing broken bulbs, fixing broken toys, scheduling appointments, keeping up with homework - all of it is on you. And, if you're like me, you work too. Is your house realistically going to be neat and tidy? Would you yell at me and tell me I suck if you saw that my house was a mess? Of course not. You're doing the best you can. And so am I. And you know what? Sometimes, often even, my house is a total wreck.

Being a single mom is messy. There are days when I run around like a chicken with my head cut off and fall into bed looking at the mess of stuff I didn't get done. It's exhausting.

I'm not telling you that you shouldn't try to keep your house clean. When your house is cluttered and dirty, you may feel cluttered and dirty too. Of course, it's important to take care of those chores as best you can. You can't abandon them completely. But it's a little like a riddle — you know you should do it but there's only so much you can realistically do. If you can hire help, do it — I do when I can and I feel zero guilt about that. If your kids are at an age where they can help with chores, create a system that encourages them to help you — it's good for them too. But no amount of help ever seems to be enough.

Be gentle with yourself and try to make peace with the mess. It's okay if your floors have a thin layer of dirt on them now and again or if the laundry piles up more than it used to. Right now, I am fishing through baskets of clean laundry to find clothes because I haven't found the time to put away the laundry recently. I can never seem to keep up with the laundry. Once I put it away, it feels like there's more to do. And that's okay because I feel certain that my kids will not remember how hard it was to find a clean pair of matching socks when they were growing up. They will not be scarred by my inability to fold.

Exercise: Ignore the mess.

That's all. Just this once. Give yourself a moment of peace and permission to ignore the mess.

MOTHER'S DAY MIGHT SUCK.

My first divorced Mother's Day was not a happy day for me. Mother's Day was a day without breaks or help or fancy meals. I didn't feel showered with affection or gratitude and in fact endured my oldest daughter's anger and hostility for much of the day while my little ones threw tantrums. Hopping on Facebook to see other moms posting their breakfast in bed or weekend family fun felt like pouring salt in a wound that went right through to my core, leaving me feeling hollow and worthless. It didn't just suck. It was excruciating. I hated Mother's Day. It was awful.

If your Mother's Day sucks, I want you to know you're not alone. And if it doesn't, enjoy it.

If your first Mother's Day as a single mom is on the horizon, think ahead. Find a way to create time for self-care. My ex enjoyed a 5-mile hike on Mother's Day while I took care of my kids by myself all day. I wish I had asked for someone to come over to make the day a little easier. If I had thought about it ahead of time, maybe I would have. That's why I am telling you, so you can think about it ahead of time and make a plan.

Learn from my mistakes. I don't get extra points for having suffered on Mother's Day. All I got was a shitty Mother's Day.

And by the way, no Mother's Day has been as shitty as that first one for me or my kids. We have figured it out. Which means if you have a terrible Mother's Day, it doesn't mean Mother's Day will always so be terrible.

BEING A SINGLE MOM (OR DAD) IS HARD. MANY THINGS IN LIFE WORTH DOING ARE.

Sometimes, people tell me things like, "It must be hard being a single mom." It feels good, because yeah, it is. It's hard. I just took my twins to the grocery store and dealt with two argumentative toddlers, one of whom kept trying to bite me in the check-out line. And I managed to get groceries. My two toddlers never look up at me and say, "I am sorry I bit you and called you names. You are doing an amazing job and I love you." No, that doesn't happen. Validation from someone, anyone, feels good because I don't have a partner who hugs me at the end of the day and backs me up.

Being a single mom is brutal. But I have to believe it's worth it. My son may wipe his snot on my shirt and use me as his tissue, but it's worth it to get a hug from him after a nap. Getting to raise these little critters is exhausting. And getting to raise these little critters is also a gift. I get to be a part of their little lives. I get to watch them grow into the people they are becoming and even help shape who they are going to be (hopefully, for the better and not only for the worse). It's kind of freaking unbelievable although I must admit, I don't always feel the eternal gratitude for it that I do in this very moment.

In those times, when it feels hard, when it feels impossible, even, take those deep breaths. At least four. Ten if you can.

Then when you're done, look around. Notice what you see.

You're okay. In this moment, you are okay.

You know what? You are better than okay.

You are badass.

You are a badass mom.

And if you don't have kids and you're just trying to make it through this divorce, you're badass too.

Divorce is not easy.

Kids or no kids.

You got this.

Anytime you lose sight of that (and if you are like me, you will quite often), take those deep breaths, look around and remind yourself.

You are an incredible badass.

That's what single moms are.

Exercise: I am a badass.

Look yourself in the mirror, in the eyes. Tell yourself "You are badass. I am badass." And then smile at your badass self, because you are.

SECTION 4:

DATING

Survival Skills

HELP, THERE'S AN INSECURE TEENAGE GIRL TRAPPED INSIDE OF ME AND SHE'S ANNOYING.

The last time I dated, I was 19 years old. And now I am dating again, and I am discovering something I really don't like. Dating brings out the insecure teenage girl in me that I didn't even know was there. It's beyond embarrassing.

If this has not happened to you, hooray. But if it has, I want you to know you are not alone. I have checked in with other newly single divorced moms and they report similar captive insecure teenage girls taking over their brain circuitry. They lie to themselves, just like you do, and say things like, "I'm not going to chase him." They try to make themselves sound all empowered. And they are. And they also hide a similarly insecure teenage girl who totally wants to chase him. The good news is that we are intelligent enough to overpower this obnoxious voice with sound reason and intelligent action. The bad news is that she's there for the long haul.

Dating brings up insecurity. If you haven't been single in a long time, you haven't felt that in a long time. It's new. At least it was to me. What I tried to do is notice it, be mindful of it, and have a sense of humor about it. That worked sometimes. Sometimes, not so much.

But I also set boundaries for myself so my inner secure teenager can't do too much damage. Boundaries like: If I am feeling needy and I want to send a text, I put it in a note on my phone and wait until I feel less needy to decide if I should send it. I am safe and careful with dating. If I meet someone online and I am thinking about going out with them, I google them by phone number or name. I have been surprised by some of what I have found doing this — felons, dick pics — and I don't go out with them if anything comes up.

Be careful out there and look after that teenage girl. She needs the adult in you to keep her safe. Google his number, meet in a public place, don't let him pick you up, tell a friend who you're meeting and where you're going.

Exercise: How do you protect that teenage girl from doing stupid stuff?

Take a moment to reflect on the boundaries you need to keep that teenage girl inside of you from making your life harder. What boundaries do you need to set in terms of texting, meeting, dating, and talking to prospects?

DATING IS FUN. AND DATING SUCKS. MORE THAN YOU THINK, BOTH WAYS.

I have rewritten this chapter so many times depending on my mood and what funny story I have to share. But I am done rewriting it. Online dating is a book — a different book. For the purposes of your divorce and this period of your life, this is what you need to know:

Dating has changed. Of course, if you weren't in a twenty-year relationship, these changes might not feel quite as drastic. However, what I gather from clients and friends is that dating has changed exponentially even in the last few years.

Online dating makes it easy to line up dates. This is true for men and women. And this is fun. But the ease makes people take it less seriously too. It's pretty weird out there. You can swipe on people to like them or not like them. Guys who were too timid to approach women are suddenly empowered by the anonymity of their screen to approach whomever they please, sometimes quite brazenly. The rules have changed. Assume people you date are dating and swiping on many — and you should do the same.

People do weird things and inappropriate things because they feel shielded by their electronic screen. Some can be rude and disrespectful. Some just want to sleep with you and have become quite skilled at sleeping with many — it's too easy now.

DTF means 'down to fuck', by the way. You should know that. FWB means 'friends with benefits'. Some men text dick pics and apparently there are women out there who will text pictures of themselves naked too. Not trying to scare you but prepare you.

Collect your funny stories and enjoy them. Try not to take it too seriously unless you meet someone worth taking seriously and hold on to your sense of humor. But be careful too. People are often not who they say they are, and their intentions are not always pure. Online dating makes for a strange field of play. Learn the rules cautiously and make rules of your own to keep yourself safe and comfortable out there.

The landscape is rich with options to connect with others and their popularity shifts rapidly. Ask other singles in your area what apps people are using where you live. Of course, the best way to understand dating websites is to hop on and check it out — you can always delete an app if you don't like it.

Beware, it's easy to get caught up in a swift game of slutty swiping. It becomes like candy crush and suddenly, depressing bathroom and gym selfies of men you don't want to date sucked away your time. It's easy to get lost and it doesn't feel good when it's over. Be gentle with yourself.

And be careful. Rates of sexually transmitted disease (STD) among recently divorced women are high for a number of reasons. We are not as worried about getting pregnant so we may forgo the condom. Big mistake. Physiological changes in the vaginal walls of middle-aged women make us more susceptible to STDs. Be as responsible as you expect your kids to be. You are not immune to STDs and in fact, it's more the opposite. Be careful.

Bottom line, if someone makes you feel icky, you can do better. Don't ever forget that you can always do better.

I say this with absolute confidence because you will always be there for you. And this divorce is a ginormous hurdle toward proving that to yourself.

If you feel discouraged with online dating and delete the apps, you are not alone. I did that a lot of times. However, the last time I did it was a year ago when I met somebody on a dating site who was worth taking seriously. I'm enjoying an incredibly healthy, happy relationship with him. It does happen. There are good men out there — I know because I found one.

Exercise: Create a code of ethics when dating.

What boundaries are important to you in terms of dating? Think about how you hold on to your integrity and feel good about dating. Does this mean you can't date men who hug drugged tigers in their profile pics? You are worth it. You don't have to compromise your integrity to date so think about what that means to you.

BEFORE YOU DATE SERIOUSLY AGAIN, DO THIS.

You're going to need a couple lists before you start dating.

Look at your dead marriage and think about the qualities you needed your ex to have that he did not. Think about the reasons your marriage didn't work and what you must have in your next partner in order for your next relationship to work. Think about qualities that are absolute deal breakers for you and write them down. To get you started in the right direction, here are some common deal breakers: Must be empathetic, kind, financially stable, has friends and hobbies, active, sociable, flexible. Other common deal breakers: Can't be an addict, smoke, have anger management issues, own more than three pets. Don't take these as your own. Find the ones that fit with your lived experience. This is <u>your</u> deal breakers list. You're going to need it one day.

Make sure that your list of deal breakers includes the qualities of safe people and excludes qualities that you find unsafe or intolerable. You deserve a safe relationship. Examples of deal breakers designed to screen for safe people are: Actions matching up with words, polite to wait staff, and having healthy relationships with friends and/or family. If someone's actions don't match their words, they are rude to wait staff or they have no healthy relationships, those are all huge red flags that something is amiss. They will not be consistent and you can't trust them. They may be rude to you or disrespectful. If they have no healthy relationships in their life, they are likely not capable of healthy relationships.

Next, write a list of qualities that you would like to find in a partner. These are not deal breakers, but ideals. Common qualities include: Funny, intelligent, physically fit, tall (or short). Again, use the ones that fit with your lived experience and the qualities you find most attractive.

When you start dating, if you discover early on that the person you are dating doesn't live up to one of your deal breakers, end it immediately. Additionally, you may find that you start to see deal breakers and the qualities that attract you more readily because you know what it is you're looking for.

These lists set you up for success in finding your next relationship. They're important. They're your compass. I often have single clients make these lists and it's a little bit like a vision board — suddenly, they find someone who fits their needs. And I have my lists too, tucked away in a note on my phone — and I used mine too.

Don't forget that you have the lists. Look back at them. Consult them. Hold yourself accountable to them.

Exercise: Create your deal breakers list and your qualities that you would like to find list.

Spend time with these lists. Make sure you consider factors like safe versus unsafe people and qualities that will tip you off. Keep it somewhere safe. These lists are important when you start to date.

YOU CAN HAVE A FLING IF YOU WANT TO.

Kissing a boy again without any baggage is fun. When you were married, this was off the table. It's not anymore. Don't let your kids see it, but if you want to have a fling, do it. You can.

This is one of the perks of divorce. Don't squander it. Don't feel guilty for it. Enjoy it. Having a meaningless physical relationship with a surfer nearly a decade younger than you might be fun. Just saying.

And if this doesn't align with your religious or moral beliefs, feel free to disregard. I'm not meaning to offend you. You have to make choices that feel right to you.

Exercise: Reflect on your dating history.

Think about the choices you made in terms of dating before you were married and the choices you want to make moving forward. What do you want? Be honest with yourself. It's okay if you're simply looking to have fun for now.

BEWARE OF OXYTOCIN.

For evolutionary reasons, women are programmed to want a provider. When we cuddle, a hormone called oxytocin is released in our bodies and it feels really good.

It feels like love. It is NOT love.

We want it, we crave it and we don't want it to go away when we get a taste of it. Men are not wired the same way. From an evolutionary perspective, it serves him better to spread his seed far and wide. He doesn't feel the pull that you do. He doesn't get the blast of oxytocin that you do. It's okay to feel that rush and to enjoy it, but don't mistake it for more than it is and be mindful of it. You don't love this man you've known for a short time. Slow down. Don't get all clingy. Let it be what it is and nothing more unless it turns into something more.

He is not your provider.

You are.

Exercise: Are you craving touch? Do something about it.

If you notice that you're craving touch, schedule a massage, a pedicure or hug a friend. Our human desire to touch and be touched is real. Make sure you're getting that need met without putting yourself in a position desperate enough to be touched by men who aren't right for you. I go to the foot massage place in my neighborhood for an excellent $25 full-body massage when I notice that I am craving touch.

YOUR PICKER MAY NEED TUNING SO BE CAREFUL.

You picked someone who was not a good fit for you. Be careful out there so that you don't do it again.

I picked my husband. I have spent a lot of time contemplating how and why that happened, and the honest truth is that something in me is broken. Sure, I can complain about him and how he hurt me, but that doesn't change the fact that I chose him. I maintained a relationship with him for twenty years. No, not all men are like my ex. However, I know I need to be cautious and question my judgment every step of the way because I picked him and I had no idea I was doing it.

While my picker is not the most reliable, I do have friends who picked excellent husbands. I use their judgment as back-up and made sure they met and approved of the man I am currently dating.

I cannot tell you how often I see people move on to other relationships, thinking that they have chosen someone totally different because they have other personality traits or interests, only to realize years later that they did it again. Some people in the field of psychology believe that we unintentionally choose people with whom we think we can work out our childhood baggage. For instance, the little girl who is constantly begging for daddy's approval and validation and never getting it often chooses a partner who is unable to provide the approval and validation she so desperately wants. Oddly, that feeling of rejection feels strangely comfortable and the work required to change that dynamic is uncomfortable, so she inadvertently repeats this dynamic over and over again in partners who are all completely different from each other but alike in this one critical way.

This is one of the many reasons I go to therapy. I am intensely aware now that my judgment is not where it needs to be in terms of the men I choose. I am not going to let that bite me again, but it means I have to be very careful. When I work with women who are dating, I ask them the difficult questions. I help them look for red flags and consider behaviors or actions in the men they are dating that they might be tempted to overlook. I also help clients examine their patterns based on their own childhood experiences that draw them to men who are likely not right for them and why they find them attractive anyway. I have relied upon my own therapist to help me examine these same issues. Sometimes I am too hard on myself and I need a therapist to help me see it clearly.

Exercise: How do you feel about your picker?

Just take some time to reflect on your own picker. How do you safeguard against picking badly? Do you consult with friends? Do you process with a therapist? How will you make sure you don't pick the wrong guy?

BE ALONE. NOTICE HOW IT FEELS.

After realizing that on-line dating became an obsessive gaming app for me, I took down my dating profiles for a long while. Online dating wasn't about dating anymore. It was about some twisted game that hijacked my brain circuitry in ways that didn't feel right to me and battered my self-esteem. Several months later, I put them back on my phone, but I needed time to reflect on what was happening at the time.

I began to feel itchy for texts from interested prospects. My mood tanked when I didn't get them and soared when I did. I didn't like it. When I polled other single friends, I discovered this phenomenon is common. I needed to step back.

When the texts stopped, I felt the loneliness and fear of being alone settle in. For me, that was part of the grieving process. I needed to allow myself to be completely alone, even though it was uncomfortable.

I think that for most people, learning to be alone is a critical life skill because it makes being with someone who is not great not worth it. And it challenges us to face difficult feelings and fears. If you have not been alone, I encourage you try it. Not forever. Just for a while.

While it brought up difficult feelings for me, it also left me feeling empowered. I like time by myself. I sometimes crave it. Additionally, it allowed me to focus without distraction on some of my goals. Like finishing this book. And building my therapy practice. And planning quality time with my kids and friends I value.

My eye was on the prize. Which was not a man. It's me. I had more space to recover me. And I'm not so bad.

Exercise: Make space for you. Allow yourself to be alone.

Spend time alone focusing on you. What would it look like to take a break from online dating (if that's where you are)? What does it feel like to be alone? What feelings do you notice? If they are difficult or uncomfortable, rest assured, they will pass.

You are the prize. Not some dude online. You. Take a moment to write down five qualities you like about you. People hate doing this, but it's important. Please do it. And if you want to write more, extra credit. Fill the page. You're more amazing than you think and you don't need some guy to tell you that for it to be true.

THE ANSWER IS NOT A MAN (OR WOMAN).

When I was using the dating apps and I felt stressed out about my divorce or work or my kids or whatever, I often lost time on those dating apps. There's a reason for this. Thinking about boys was so much simpler than thinking about selling my house, supporting my family on my own, or any of the seemingly unbearable subjects that divorce brings to the surface. Swiping through boys on some dating app felt a lot lighter.

When I found myself thinking about men, I did my best to remind myself that it's not real. It's diversion. The idea, the fantasy, that any man is going to fix any of this is useless. This doesn't mean a relationship can't be meaningful and fulfilling. It means a relationship with a man isn't going to solve all of my problems.

Nobody can save me but me. It's all on my shoulders.

I can do this. I don't need anyone to save me. I can enjoy a man, appreciate a man, but I will never need one. Not now. Not ever. The relationship I have

now is incredibly fulfilling and meaningful to me —
and I don't need <u>him</u> to complete me. I am not with him
because I need him. I am with him because I want to
be. And I feel strength and love for myself and for him
in this.

When you find yourself imagining a future in
which your life is magically fixed by another person,
knock it off. You don't need another person to fix you.
You are the person who fixes you and you are enough.
The more you are able to embrace that, the happier you
will be and the more you will be able to appreciate the
men who do come into your life.

Sometimes, it's hard to shift gears and see the
world this way. Growing up with old school Disney
messages about love and relationships or
family/cultural messages that landing a man is key are
hard to shake. They may leave you feeling as though
you are not whole without a man. Don't be a slave to
these messages. You can notice them and choose to let
them go. It's much harder than it sounds though so be
gentle with yourself.

Exercise: Do you have a rescue fantasy?

Have you fantasized about someone rescuing you and fixing your life? Where did this fantasy come from? What perpetuates it? What would it be like to let it go? For a moment, create a fantasy in which you rescue you and fix your life. What does the fantasy look like? What keeps you from making it happen?

SECTION 5:

THRIVING AFTER DIVORCE

Making Room for a Brighter Future and Moving On

GRIEVING YOUR MARRIAGE — WHAT DOES THAT EVEN MEAN????

Denial. Anger. Bargaining. Depression. Acceptance. This is what it means to grieve.

You may notice yourself cycle through these different stages at a neck-breaking pace or you may notice yourself cycle through them slowly. They do not follow any chronological order and there is no graduation from any of the stages. Sadly, just because you've stopped feeling so depressed and have started to feel some acceptance does not mean that you won't find yourself experiencing depression or anger or denial again. There's no rhyme or reason, no way to predict it or stop it. The only way to the other side of grief is through it. And yet through it, for some, feels impossible and intolerable and so they find ways to numb.

Often people try to escape grief. They numb out with drugs, alcohol, food, or behaviors like sex, gambling or shopping that can become destructive when used compulsively as an escape. But the escape doesn't last and often brings about a whole different set of problems. If you are noticing that your attempts to escape are leading to sabotaging behaviors, be careful and consider reaching out for help.

Tolerating the emotions that come with grief is not easy but understanding that it's part of the grieving process helps. If you feel irrationally angry with someone who does not deserve your fury (like the cashier who got your order wrong or the telemarketer who wouldn't give up), notice it. The anger is likely fueled by grief. Notice what the denial, anger, bargaining, depression and acceptance feel like and be compassionate with yourself. It's not easy.

No matter how your marriage ended, you once walked down an aisle with your ex and said, "I do." This was not how you thought it would end. Even if you are relieved to be getting a divorce as I am, you have to grieve a loss. You are losing any chance of the marriage you hoped for with the person you promised to spend the rest of your life with.

It's a real loss. It makes sense to grieve. Allow yourself to grieve it. Notice what comes up for you. Be gentle with yourself.

Exercise: Examine your grief.

Think about the stages of grief listed above and reflect on examples of how they have come up for you. Have you felt the denial — this isn't really happening, anger, bargaining, maybe if you do XYZ this will all be different, depression/sadness, or acceptance - come up for you? How are you coping? Have you tried to escape in ways that are destructive?

FAREWELL
TO THE ENERGY VAMPIRES.
TAKE BACK YOUR LOST ENERGY.

While my ex was actually a pretty supportive guy in his own way when it came to my goals and aspirations, he also sucked my energy, emotional and otherwise, beyond dry in ways I did not even realize at the time. I spent so much energy and time managing him that I had nothing left for me. At the end of the day, I vegged out with him rather than apply myself to my goals and aspirations the way I could have. I contentedly watched hours of television that I didn't care much about. I spent so much emotional energy trying to connect with my partner, hold him up and make my marriage work, that I didn't even know how much energy it was draining from me then. A repertoire of mindless TV shows filled my downtime because that's all I had the energy for. Meanwhile, my goals slipped away unnoticed. I had given so much of myself to everyone else — being a good mom, good friend, good daughter, good wife — that there was nothing left for me.

This is a common struggle for women, and some men, who are often taught to put others' needs ahead of their own and come to believe that anything else is selfish. But that energy is precious, and we deserve to take care of ourselves as much as anyone else. Doing so allows us to show up and be present for others in a way that's meaningful and connective.

I took all that energy I had poured into my marriage back the day I told him to get the hell out. I had no idea how much energy that was until I began to recover. My marriage was the greatest energy vampire of all. And once it was over, my life changed.

At night, I get my house in order. I write. I get stuff done. It's not only the actual time I spent with him that I am regaining. It's the physical, psychological and emotional energy spent. I can put it elsewhere. I am writing more and building my career. Since my marriage ended, I have completed my licensure and taken over and grown my own private practice which is now thriving. I went from being an intern making a meager income to becoming a business owner and reputable therapist in my community. I am hanging photos of my kids in my house that I never got around to hanging, and planning trips with them. I am putting those resources lost to my marriage elsewhere, and it feels fantastic.

Exercise: Reclaim your energy.

Draw a box and in it, make a list of all the energy you put into your marriage — cooking, cleaning, therapy, talking, fighting, supporting. Color that box red. Think about all of the resources you lost to your failing marriage and put it in that bloody red box.

Now draw arrows to a much bigger box, a limitless blue box. In that blue box, create a list of everything you'd like to put more energy into, like family events, career, kids, and hobbies. Fill it - let it overflow. This is where you are going. Letting go of your marriage and the energy you poured into it has paved the way toward infinite possibility. Look at that box and take the time to reflect on all of the ways your newfound energy can fuel you and your growth.

DRAW THE ROADMAP TO YOUR BROKEN MARRIAGE SO YOU DON'T GO THERE AGAIN.

You got yourself here. No matter what your husband did, you made the choices that landed you in your marriage. My husband did unspeakable things while we were married, but I chose him, and I need to know how and why that happened. As much as I would like to believe he was not the same person back when I first met him, the truth is that I am not the same person I was when I first met him and I didn't see him clearly. I ignored and overlooked the pieces I didn't want to see.

Here's a very simplified version of my roadmap to give you an idea of how this works: Dad diagnosed with cancer when I was 15. I became very good at taking care of him. He died when I was 16. Mother then went through cancer, survived and moved away. Lived alone senior year of high school, and by then, I was very skilled at taking care of other people and myself. Summer after freshman year of college, I felt very alone. I met my now-ex while waiting tables and felt that because his father had also died around the same time as mine (one month before, actually), he understood me.

This is called trauma bonding, where we feel that someone who has been through a similar trauma will understand our trauma and the actual trauma becomes the glue of the relationship. He was not good at taking care of himself, so my skills at taking care of people created a perfect storm for a codependent relationship that felt comfortable to us both. He was charming. My mother told me she believed I had met my 'soulmate'. I ignored red flags I didn't want to see. I see them all now looking back, though. His disdain early in our relationship when I cried was a sign of deeper wounds that impacted his ability to be present for me when I was hurting. I felt unable to share my feelings with him because I was afraid of triggering his anger — another red flag - but I convinced myself my feelings were wrong, too much and not acceptable.

By the time I started to catch him in the bigger lies and betrayals, I owned him as family and believed he could be better. He said he would, and my codependent ways were fed by my need to fix him. I think I became a therapist thinking maybe I could fix him, but what I learned is that the only person I could fix was myself. I didn't do him any favors by trying to fix him. Actually, I cut him off at the knees. My constant managing of him made him never have to manage himself, and he was less capable of doing so as a result of my constant 'help'. I'm still a work-in-progress but so much happier with who I am now than who I was along this road.

There's more to this story, but those are the crucial turns. You need to know your crucial turns too — not to punish yourself but to make your story have meaning.

It's important for me to see the role I played in making this happen so that I don't walk this road again. I am mindful of choices I made in the past that got me here, and I pay attention when they resemble the choices I make in the present so that I can steer another direction.

Exercise: Create your roadmap.

I highly recommend finding your roadmap for how you got here too. It took me years and a lot of therapy to figure mine out, so don't distress if you don't already know how you got here. If this exercise leads to a blank page, that means you have some digging to do.

Be gentle to yourself but also take responsibility. It's not about assigning blame — it's about creating a different roadmap for yourself moving forward. You don't know how to avoid this road unless you know how you got here in the first place.

SOMETIMES IT HURTS LIKE HELL.

There are times when I feel confident, secure and happy. Those are good times.

But there are times when I don't.

There are times when the wreckage of my divorce feels like a dark cloud no matter what I do. I am writing this chapter on one of those days. It's hard for me to write. I want to do nothing. I want to sink into bed and watch TV and sleep and hope it will all go away or feel better when I wake up.

Today is a Sunday. I am spending it as the solo adult, just me and my kids who outnumber me greatly. I am sick. I am tired. I have no reinforcement. I took them to an empty parking lot to ride their bikes, and while I struggled to keep them all rounded up and safe, all I could see were happy families strolling by. I saw dads out with their kids, enjoying time with them. But it was just me with my kids. There are days when I have no adult contact at all. There are days when it's solely me and these irrational little creatures and their messes, and my life feels like it's about keeping them happy and fed and then cleaning up after them when it's all said and done and listening while they yell at me and make more demands. Sometimes, it feels hollow and empty. Sometimes I feel sad and lonely and like I always will be.

I don't like telling you about this piece of me that I don't love to be around. But I'm sharing for a reason. You may find yourself here at some point. You may feel the sadness and the pain and have difficulty seeing anything half full. I keep thinking how different my life looks than what I wanted for myself and my kids, and that hurts so much. I even spiral into a 'why me' pity party every now and again, wondering why my friends are enjoying family vacations over the holiday break while I struggle to do this all on my own at home. And then there's the guilt — what a selfish bitch I am for even thinking these thoughts. I have three amazing healthy children. I should focus on how grateful I am to have them. Now I am starting down the path where I beat myself up for having feelings I don't like. The whole thing is a big ugly mess.

So here it is. Me at my most vulnerable and real. Going through a divorce is gut-wrenching and painful at times. Sometimes, it just hurts. I tell my clients to remember that the central nervous system runs through their entire body, not only their head, and that's why psychological pain often manifests as physical pain. I do feel physical pain right now. All over. I am hurting. There's a reason why it's called 'heartache'.

All I can say is what I say to myself at these times. I have hurt before. I am hurting now. I will hurt again. But I do not always hurt like this and I will not always hurt like this.

When you land in this place, try to remember that too.

And one more thing about this hurting place — it's okay to be here sometimes. We live in a culture where people preach that happiness is a choice and thus anything outside of it is a choice too. I call bullshit. Yes, we can make choices that make us miserable and choices that make us happy, but sometimes we feel sad or hurt and it's okay to have those feelings too. Pain and sadness are as much a part of the fabric of human existence as happiness and pleasure. If you don't ever feel the darkness, how can you expect to fully appreciate the light? It's okay to feel dark sometimes. If you stay there or it gets too dark, reach out for help. But there's nothing wrong with you for being there and don't let anybody tell you otherwise. When other people can't tolerate your difficult emotions, that's not about you — that's about them.

CREATE INTENTIONS
OR A VISION BOARD.

There is a bit of magic in this. When you write out on paper what you want to make happen in the year ahead, you put your energy there. You make it happen. The year I threw my husband out, I had written down intentions at the start of the year. On that list: Find clarity around my marriage. And that's exactly what I did.

Intentions are more powerful than you can imagine. It's not a resolution. It's about creating a plan for yourself. Do not be shy when setting intentions. Push outside of what's comfortable or even what's possible and reach for what would be incredible. Then line up the steps to get there. Break it down, what it takes to get where you want. Put the steps on your calendar. Do them. That's how you make it happen. Some, like finding clarity around my marriage, may not be about the steps that get you there so much as the awareness that it needs to happen.

Consider every aspect of your life when setting intentions — relationships, health, financial, professional, family. Imagine you can have it all and then plan it as though you will.

Decide what needs to happen in your life and then go out and make it happen. Having it in your head is not enough. Spell it out on paper — make yourself accountable to it.

Exercise: Write down your intentions or create a vision board.

Just do it. Either one. Doesn't have to be pretty. Doesn't have to be perfect.

GOODBYE LIES.
NO MORE CATS
STUCK IN RAT TRAPS.

Not all marriages that end are packed with lies, but many are. Mine was. Living with those lies, wondering what the truth might be, sucks. It's painful and exhausting. There is no clarity, only confusion.

A skilled liar also understands the art of gaslighting which feels like waterboarding in a relationship. Gaslighting is when your partner feels the shame of what they have done and, as a coping skill, diverts that attention to you, making you the crazy one who has done terrible awful things. For example, when someone accuses their partner of cheating (and they are), the cheating partner may be angry and disgusted by your lack of trust. The cheating partner's outrage might be so great that you may feel as though you have done something truly terrible by even considering that your partner is cheating even though it's true. Gaslighting works, but it's destructive and leaves the gaslit partner feeling crazy and confused.

A friend told me this story and I kind of love it. Warning, this story is a bit raunchy so if you are easily offended, you may want to skip this part. This couple had been married for a long time. They had kids. The husband started coming home late, working weekends, all of the hallmark signs. Then one night, he comes home from a late night at 'work' with blood all over his shirt. He's trying to cover it up with a flannel shirt tied around his waist, but his wife notices and asks about the blood. He came up with a whopper.

Apparently, on his way home, he saw a cat with its head stuck in a rat trap on the side of the road, so he stopped and pulled over to help the cat. He extricated the cat and took it to the vet. I mean, he couldn't leave the cat to die, could he? When his wife questioned the absurdity of the story, he was outraged and disgusted by her lack of trust and actually pretended to call the vet to check on the cat.

I believed a lot of lies myself that sound pretty absurd in hindsight. Being a sucker, falling for the lies, was exhausting and painful.

So, like me, you are probably wondering, "How did he get all that blood on his shirt?"

He was having sex with his secretary who was on her period.

It is a huge relief to live in a world without all of the lies. No more bullshit. If you're like me, living in a marriage filled with cats stuck in rat traps was exhausting. Opening the door to a life where that doesn't happen anymore is an incredible relief.

The day I told my ex I was done was the day I discovered how many cats stuck in rat traps existed in my life. It was unbearable. As terrifying as it was to step out into the unknown, it was a huge relief to know that lies would not continue to scar me. I was done. Forever. Done.

You don't have to endure the lies anymore either. No more cats stuck in rat traps. There is more peace in that than you may even realize.

Exercise: Looking back, were there instances in your marriage where your partner gaslit you?

Think about some of the lies (if there were any) that persisted in your marriage. Revisit the moments when you believed there was something wrong with you for not trusting. You're not crazy. What's it like to live a life without cats stuck in rat traps?

HELLO TRUTH. BRACE YOURSELF. REALITY MAY NOT BE PRETTY.

The lies are gone and that brings relief. However, the truth may not be so comforting. It's sometimes a harsh reality when the ex's niceties dissolve and you discover the truth about what life is going to be like after your divorce. That was true for me.

There are those stories that you hear where parents get along better after the divorce and fathers step up when they are single dads in ways that they never did while married. This may happen for you, so don't discount the possibility.

But sometimes the truth is painful. I have one friend whose ex stopped answering phone calls from their children. Her pre-teen son called his dad crying, begging him to call back and he didn't. Another friend left her palatial home and lived in a small guesthouse because her ex hid his money, filed for bankruptcy and wouldn't give her anything, despite the fact that he lived in an estate with a pool and a tennis court. I know a woman whose ex didn't move out until after he found out he got his girlfriend pregnant. She had six months to explain to her children that dad was moving, that they were getting a divorce, that dad had a new girlfriend and that they were going to have a new sibling very soon. The truth is sometimes rough.

I'm not trying to scare you with horror stories. My friend who is living in the guesthouse says she's the happiest she has ever been so even though these stories sound painful and scary, none of these women regret their decision to let go of their marriage. It's hard and painful and scary. I am relieved to not live with the weight of my marriage and yet the truth is not rainbows and unicorns. There are challenges in that too.

It's worth it, but brace yourself.

Exercise: What truths scare you?

Reflect on the truths that keep you awake at night. Just here. Just now. Put it on a piece of paper and then let it go. Don't live in fear of the truths that scare you. Look at them, be prepared for them, and then step into the light. The truth may not be as bad as you think, or it may take a different course. Stand up to your fear of the truth.

YOU NEVER DIVORCE THE SAME PERSON YOU MARRY. THAT GOES BOTH WAYS.

Take a hard look at who you are now, who you once were and who you want to be. Then be it.

When this divorce began, I felt like a victim. I wasn't sure who I was. But I made choices based on who I wanted to be.

Self-esteem comes from making honorable choices. You are the sum of the choices you make. Some of the choices you want to make are scary and uncomfortable. If you succumb to the fear and anxiety, you will not make them. However, you can make the choice to be uncomfortable. You can make the choice to be the person you want to be and live the life you want to live. It's okay to allow yourself to sit with the discomfort of taking risks and pushing outside of your comfort zone. It's not always easy, but I believe in it. If I didn't, this book would still be on my laptop and never in your hands.

The road to success is often paved with failure. Accept it, but don't let that stand in your way. Failure doesn't feel good, but if you don't risk failing, you limit how high you can go. Failure is often a bridge to opportunity and growth.

When I look back at my marriage, I can see how being comfortable in a marriage riddled with painful lies felt easier at the time than the discomfort of getting a divorce. The best choice I ever made was to get divorced, but it was terrifying. The little girl who got married in her mid-twenties is not the same woman who walked away from that very same marriage. I am proud of that.

Take stock in the risks you took to be here and the risks you will take to get where you want and need to be. Be proud of yourself. It was, is and will be no small feat.

Exercise: *Who were you that day at the altar and who are you now?*

Think back to the day you got married. Who was she? Who is she now? Take a moment to reflect and pat yourself on the back for how much you've grown.

TAKE INVENTORY
OF YOUR WOUNDS.
BE MINDFUL OF THEM.

Trusting men scares me and deep down, I struggle with the belief that my judgment is irreparably flawed. I have symptoms of PTSD including a heightened startle response, gifts from the trauma within my marriage and my divorce. I want to control everything and struggle desperately to make peace with my own imperfection because I want everything I do to be perfect, and it never is. I tend to be anxious and if I don't go for a run most days, I have a hard time managing my anxiety. I have difficulty trusting men in all aspects of my life and an even harder time trusting my own judgment.

I know these things about myself and that empowers me to face them. I often tell clients I don't have a magic wand that can make something they don't like about themselves go away for them, but I can help them change their relationship with it. That's sort of how I feel about this. I know my baggage and I have to be aware of it, like it's a passenger on the train. I'm the train. And if the passengers get unruly, the train is going to crash. Again. I have to pay attention and not let the unruly passengers drive the train anymore. I know what that wreck looks like and it's not pretty.

Notice the baggage you struggle with, and how this marriage and divorce have impacted you. Change your relationship with it. It doesn't go away. It's a part of you. It's not all of you. Make it smaller. Give it less power. Be able to laugh at it instead of fear it. Work on it, address it, be mindful of it. You are bigger. You will be okay. There are other parts of you that can safely drive the bus and calm the passengers having a harder time.

Exercise: *Assess the baggage on your train.*

What are your passengers? What do you need to be mindful of? How does your baggage impact you and in what ways could you change your relationship with it?

INVENTORY YOUR STRENGTHS.

I am strong and I am resilient, and I can manage almost anything. I am also calm, most of the time, except when both of my twins act out of control, angry, and wild at the very same time. I can keep my shit together even when it's really hard to do it. I am kind and loving and a thinker. It feels arrogant and uncomfortable to write all of this, but it's important to take an inventory of our strengths. I'm letting myself be uncomfortable so that you may feel inspired to do the same.

Tolerate the discomfort and write down your strengths. Please. It's important. And this is why:

We come from a culture where women (and some men) are often taught to downplay their strengths. But that's bullshit. Take stock of what you do well and feel proud. Feel good about your positive qualities and use them to your advantage. You need to know what they are. If this exercise is hard for you, then it's even more important that you complete it. If it's really hard, then come up with a different strength every day for a week and write it on a sticky-note on your mirror, because the pieces of you that you need the most are hiding.

Don't downplay how amazing you are. You've been there for yourself through all of this. That is huge.

Exercise: Inventory your strengths.

Make a list of all of your strengths. Don't be shy. The more, the better.

'FORGIVE AND FORGET' IS OVERRATED. OTHER ANTIDOTES TO BITTERNESS EXIST.

People say it is important to forgive and forget or else you will suffer from bitterness and never move on. I disagree. Sometimes, it's best not to forgive and forget, particularly if it leaves you feeling unsafe.

Forgiveness is a personal choice and it's not necessary to stave off bitterness. A lot of people might disagree with me, but I am giving you permission not to forgive if that's what you need to feel safe in the world.

Some of what happened during my divorce was terrifying and painful. There was a period of time when the muscles in my arm were deteriorating as a result of a pinched nerve, I had a referral to a neurosurgeon and was told that this condition would likely worsen if I did not have surgery, I was having to clear out 20 years' worth of shared stuff during the holiday season while preparing for a move with three kids, I had almost no income because I was having to care for twins who were barely four, I was struggling to keep the new business I had just gotten off the ground afloat, and the worst part: I didn't know where I was going to live or how I would secure a rental. I was terrified and overwhelmed and alone — I didn't feel safe at all.

I will never fully forgive or forget this or the ways in which the circumstances of my divorce amplified my pain during this time. And I am also not bitter. My kids and I were not homeless. I was fortunate — we made it through. A kind retired single mom took a chance on me and let me rent from her and her new husband (thank you, Stephanie and Rick) despite the fact that I had no proof of income substantial enough to afford rent. The neighbors next door were kind and welcoming (thank you, Janet and Charles). Janet brought me soup on the day I moved in. Charles came over to hang out with my kids regularly and bonded with my pup, Raja, taking her for almost daily walks. So many friends showed up and helped me through that challenging time in my life and offered me a place to stay if I truly was stuck, including friends I didn't even know well. It helped me to remember that most people are kind and good.

I didn't feel safe enough to simply forgive and forget. And I don't have to be bitter either. I'm not. Holding on to the kindness of the people who helped me keeps me from feeling bitter. I am surrounded by kindness and generosity of spirit. Love. I couldn't be more grateful. I will never forget the kindness of the people who helped me through that time in my life (there were so many). I have moved on, I feel safe, I am not bitter.

So, what I'm saying is this: If you can feel safe while forgiving and that feels important to you, forgive away. I don't object to forgiveness. And if forgiveness feels like it would leave you feeling unsafe or you're not feeling able to do it, that's okay too. As long as you are open to kindness and love elsewhere, forgiveness is not necessary to move on. I believe that because I have lived it.

Exercise: Connect to kindness and cultivate gratitude for it.

Take a moment to reflect on anyone and everyone who has made your journey easier with kindness. Reflect on the kindness that keeps you from bitterness. It's there. Even if the dark cloud keeps you from seeing it right away, if you take the time to look for it, you will see the kindness too.

WRITE A LETTER
TO YOUR FUTURE SELF.

When you write the letter to your future self, there are some important topics to cover. I know what some of them are, but I am not you and I am not walking in your exact shoes. Only you know what truly needs to be said in this letter.

Make sure that you're writing this letter on a good day. Write it on a day when you feel good about yourself and what you've overcome to get here. That's the day that you will be able to write the letter that needs to be written.

Write about why you got a divorce and what you want for yourself. Remind yourself about your strengths and what you've overcome through the process of this divorce. Make sure you are clear about what you will not tolerate in future relationships, and what you want and need to feel whole by yourself. Remind yourself about the qualities you didn't know you had before this and write about the activities, hobbies and things that bring you peace and joy.

Write this letter and keep it somewhere safe because you may need it someday. You may have a moment or a day or a week or a month where you feel uncertain about who are and where you're going.

The best person to center you is you.

Exercise: Write your letter to you.

Keep it, save it, somewhere safe and remember that it's there.

THROW A DIVORCE PARTY.

When people get married, they celebrate the start of their life together. I genuinely believe that you should also celebrate the start of your new life without your husband. The start of a new life, no matter who is in it, deserves celebration. If your marriage was as excruciating as mine, divorce is the start of a new life with the promise of more happiness than you suffered trying to find in your marriage. Besides, it's important to acknowledge great accomplishments. Navigating your way through a divorce, one of life's greatest stressors, is an enormous accomplishment.

When my divorce was finalized with the courts, I invited the women who supported me through it over for dinner. I made a cedar planked salmon, friends brought food and wine, and we remembered tales of the terrors of what I had been through and all I had survived with laughter and joy. It was a reminder of how much I gained over the course of my divorce, a deep gratitude for these incredible friendships and women who I admire deeply, and also a deep gratitude for all I had risen above and overcome to get to that table. I had so much fun at that dinner. We took a picture that night of all of them and I posted it to Facebook with a huge thank you. People thought it was my birthday. It felt like my birthday, with gifts deeper and more meaningful than I could ever express with words. I will always remember that dinner fondly.

Celebrate your divorce with your friends. Being divorced isn't something you have to be ashamed of. You had the courage to get out. If you've completed your divorce, it wasn't easy getting there. Your party doesn't have to be big or fancy, but do take the time to celebrate this even if it's a simple dinner with a friend or friends. At one time, I envisioned a huge bash with a cake with a chalk outline of a groom that bled when you cut it. That didn't happen. It didn't need to. My divorce dinner will always be special to me.

Getting here was huge. You made it. Celebrate what's to come because there's good stuff around the bend for you too.

BE SUCCESSFUL.
IT'S EASIER THAN YOU THINK.

"Success is liking yourself, liking what you do, and liking how you do it." — Maya Angelou

Months ago, I made a plan to do a terrain race with friends. It's a 5k run through obstacles including troughs of cold water, rope climbs, wall climbs, vats of mud, and various tasks like overturning giant tires along the way. As race day neared, my friends bailed. The last one bailed the night before. I almost backed out too, but I wanted to do it.

And so I did.

I woke up, I drove to the race, and I completed it. By myself. I was scared to do it alone, scared of being different than the other people there who came with tribes of friends and scared of being in a tub of freezing water with strangers. But I did it anyway.

When I was done, I felt fantastic. I made friends along the way. I made my way through mud and over barriers and walls. I made it to the end and tried everything along the way including the monkey bars over freezing cold water (which I fell in).

I felt successful. I liked what I did. I liked how I did it and that I got up and did it alone when everyone else bailed.

This is not a huge success story by any means, but not every success has to be a huge success.

Enjoy your success. The small ones are important too. Look for opportunities to create more success in your life. It feels good and you deserve that.

Exercise: What are your small successes? What are your big ones?

Take a moment to think about what your successes are. What successes do you want? Think of opportunities to like yourself, like what you do, and like how you do it. Jump on them. Enjoy them.

CONGRATULATIONS.
YOU CAN SURVIVE ANYTHING.
AND NOW YOU KNOW.

There is a secret that I saved for the last chapter and it's critical. There are two pieces to it. You may have realized it already and it may not feel profound at all, but it is profound, especially if you take it to heart.

First and foremost, you must never stop training. This divorce is one fight in a lifetime of many more to come. They may not be battles as arduous as this and you may in fact enjoy some of the battles yet to come. The harder you train and the harder you fight for the pieces of yourself that you value, the more worth you will assign to what you're fighting for and the fuller you will feel along the way.

Second, you will be okay. You will always be okay. No matter what comes your way, you can survive it. You can thrive through it. There is nothing easy about divorce and about the journey to untangle your life from someone you once loved and trusted to share your life with. It's hard. It's exhausting. And you are making it.

If you can make it through this, you can make it through anything.

All of the life skills you learned along the way and training you've endured and continue to challenge yourself with has connected you to a strength you may not have felt fully until now. But from now on, you will know it is there. It will always be there, and nobody can ever take that away. You walked away from your marriage because you deserved more (and that is true even if you are not the one who chose to end it).

And now you know the truth of it — <u>you</u> are more.

You survived this. You can survive anything.

EPILOGUE: IT GETS EASIER.

As I have had some time to recover from my divorce, I want to share something with you.

It gets so much easier.

Yes, there are still battles and disappointments. But every day does not feel like a battle. The ex has faded into the background — he is easier to deal with. He fights with me less. If I am being completely honest, to his credit, he actually treats me kindly and respectfully most of the time. I am still guarded and cautious, but this makes co-parenting way easier and he takes up little space in my life.

The boundaries are still there — don't ever set them aside or forget the past. I have engaged in text battles that I regretted, and I am conscious to keep my distance even when he seems kind.

I have moved on. I have my feet on the ground financially and I am proud of the home I have built for my children. It took a lot of work to get here and that makes it even more meaningful. I am incredibly grateful.

We are going to be okay.

And by we, I mean me and my family, and also you and yours.

You are invited…

Inspire others going through this — take a selfie of your new bad-ass divorce-surviving self and post it to Instagram with #HealingThroughDivorce and/or tag me @WhitneyBoole — you inspire me too. Find me on Instagram, Facebook, and Twitter:

https://www.facebook.com/wboole/
https://www.facebook.com/groups/healthroughdivorce/
https://www.instagram.com/whitneyboole/
https://twitter.com/whitneyboole

And I invite you to join the community of bad-ass divorce-survivors in my private Facebook group, 'You Got This: Healing Through Divorce'. I would like to thank all of the inspirational humans in that group for supporting each other and me as we make our divorce the start of a new happier, healthier chapter in our lives.

Wishing you love, laughter and happiness in your new life!

- Whitney

Resources

Here are some books that helped me and may help you too:

The Language of Letting Go: Daily Meditations on Codependency, Melody Beattie (2009) Hazelden Publishing.

The Life Changing Magic of Tidying Up: The Japanese Art of Decluttering and Organization, Marie Kondo (2014) Ten Speed Press.

Splitting: Protecting Yourself While Divorcing Someone with Borderline or Narcissistic Personality Disorder, Randy Kreger and Bill Eddy (2011) New Harbinger Publications.

The Gifts of Imperfection: Let Go of Who You Think You're Supposed to Be and Embrace Who You Are, Brené Brown (2010) Hazelden Publishing.

Intuitive Eating: A Revolutionary Program That Works, Evelyn Tribole and Elyse Resch (2019) St. Martin's Griffin, 3rd ed.

Acknowledgements

Thank you to my children — Riley, Wesley, and Wren. They made my marriage and my divorce completely and totally worth it. I am so grateful for my wild children who inspire me daily.

Thank you to my mom, Nolia Boole who has always supported me.

Thank you to my dad, Robert Whitney Boole — he gave me enough support in the time I had him to last a lifetime.

Thank you to my amazing friends and family for helping me clean out my garage (literally and figuratively) and supporting me through my divorce every step of the way even when I was bitter and hurting and not at my best — Maggie Ding, Danielle Naftulin, Erica Kim, Janine Hill, Loretta Mills, Betty Abe, Kathy Moura, Patty Pinanong, Heather Elkin, Emily Watts, Bu Wang, Jenny Knotts, Laurie Cooley, Mandy Cavan, Cinnamon Howard, Sepideh Saremi, Melinda Newell, Anna Prikl, Rosetta Borgic, Lisa Boole, Terri Slemmons. Thank you, Callie Martin, for reading everything I write and for showing up to support me along this journey. Thank you to my "group" for your support — Susan, Kerry, Mandy, Linda, Erin, Emily, Genevive, Nicole. Thank you Charles, Janet and AJ Payne, and Stephanie and Rick Orcutt for making my first home after my divorce a healing house. There are so many more friends who have supported me, and I am so grateful — you know who you are.

Thank you to Michael Margolin, the best coach ever, who gives me weekly vacations, perfect coffee, and support that feels magical.

Thank you to everyone who helped make this happen — Mari Lee, Dan Blanks, Yvonne Kohano — if it weren't for you, nobody would have ever seen this book but me... and Callie.

Thank you to every therapist who helped me on my recovery journey through my marriage and my divorce — Jenner Bishop, Marnie Breecker, Brenda Beardsley, Alex Katehakis— you made me want to be a therapist and I love what I do.

A special shout out to all the brave women and men in my 'You Got This: Healing Through Divorce' Support Group on Facebook — you inspire me and amaze me with your willingness to support each other despite coming from different locations, upbringings and life experiences. You have nothing in common and you have everything in common, and you show up and remind me, and each other, of the kindness in humanity through the generosity of your love for one another.

And finally thank you to my ex-husband for giving me incredible children and continuing to show up for them. The pain of our marriage and divorce spurred growth and transformation in me and I am genuinely grateful for that.

About the Author

Whitney Boole is a therapist, coach and writer in private practice in Hermosa Beach, CA. She provides therapy for individuals and couples, and she believes pain fuels growth and empowerment. She is also a single mother with three kids, including ridiculously wild twins who climb everything and leave uncapped markers everywhere they go. She runs a Facebook Group for people healing through divorce and is building more resources for those struggling with the trauma of divorce. For more information on Whitney, please visit her website at www.whitneyboole.com.

For more information on Whitney's upcoming events and to learn more about her workshops and programs, follow her on her website and on Facebook, Instagram and Twitter:

https://www.facebook.com/wboole/
https://www.facebook.com/groups/healthroughdivorce/
https://www.instagram.com/whitneyboole/
https://twitter.com/whitneyboole

CPSIA information can be obtained
at www.ICGtesting.com
Printed in the USA
LVHW101422290320
651550LV00008B/278